Over the past thirty years, retail structure has been subject to a dramatic and ongoing transʃ the emergence of large-scale specialised shops in city cen by well-known architectural David Chipperfield and Herː

Boutiques and Other Reː aiming to investigate the hiː of interior architecture. The book begins with a collection of essays presenting a critical and theoretical dimension to retail design philosophy. These are followed by interviews with top boutique designers and a series of 16 case studies spanning from 1891 to 2004 which demonstrate how boutique design has evolved in the face of cultural, social and economic changes.

Illustrated throughout with a wealth of photographs and line drawings, this book is an innovative and important contribution to architectural and interior design theory literature.

David Vernet is an architect practicing in several European countries. An Assistant Professor at the Chair of Architectural Design and Interiors (Faculty of Architecture, TU Delft) from 2003 until 2006, he was involved in teaching multidisciplinary subjects, namely performance architecture and retail design. He is currently involved in promoting architectural policies on an European level.

Leontine de Wit is an architect, interior designer and Assistant Professor at the Chair of Architectural Design and Interiors (Faculty of Architecture, TU Delft.) In 1998, she published a book on School-Housing flexible designs. She is currently teaching retail design and researching the interdisciplinary relations between interior design and industrial design.

v

Boutiques and Other Retail Spaces

Interior Architecture series

Christoph Grafe, series editor

Interiors play a significant role in the patterns of changing use and meaning in contemporary cities. Often designed as short-term proposals in existing (and often former industrial or commercial) buildings, their designers are able to respond flexibly to larger developments on an urban and global scale, both following fashions and trends and establishing them. In the design discipline, there is a high level of awareness of new developments in the wider cultural field, including the visual arts, popular visual culture, advertising and media, that other disciplines within the architectural profession sometimes lack.

At the same time, the study of interiors is a largely untheorized field, operating mainly outside the traditional territory of academic thought. This series aims to investigate the historical, theoretical and practical aspects of interiors by subjecting the results of current design activity and historical precedents to academic examination, discussing them at the level of technical solutions (light, materials and services), and against a wider cultural and historic background. All volumes contain a series of critical articles, texts by practitioners and documentation of key projects which have been selected to illustrate both their place in the history of design and the architectural solutions employed by their designers. The volumes in the Interior Architecture series can be used as a handbook for the practitioner and as a critical introduction to the history of material culture and architecture.

Forthcoming title
Cafés and Bars
The architecture of public display
Christoph Grafe and Franziska Bollerey

Routledge
Taylor & Francis Group
NEW YORK AND LONDON

Boutiques and Other Retail Spaces

The Architecture of seduction

Edited by David Vernet
and Leontine de Wit

INTERIOR ARCHITECTURE

First published 2007 by Routledge
2 Park Square, Milton Park, Abingdon, Oxon, OX14 4RN

Simultaneously published in the USA and Canada by Routledge
711 Third Avenue, New York, NY 10017

Routledge is an imprint of the Taylor & Francis Group, an informa
business

Design concept by Claudia Schenk
Typeset in Akkurat and Chaparral by Florence Productions Limited

British Library Cataloguing in Publication Data
A catalogue record for this book is available from the British Library

Library of Congress Cataloging- in-Publication Data
A catalog record for this book has been requested

ISBN10 0-415-36321-7 (hbk)
ISBN10 0-415- 36322-5 (pbk)

ISBN13 978-0-415-36321-1 (hbk)
ISBN13 978-0-415-36322-8 (pbk)
ISBN13 978-0-203-01359-5 (ebk)

Contents

Illustration credits   vii

Notes on contributors   ix

Acknowledgements   x

Foreword   xi

01   **The boutique and the mass market**   01
Mark Pimlott

02   **The shop as market space: the commercial**   16
qualities of retail architecture
Sophie Dubuisson-Quellier

03   **The vicissitudes of the boutique: introduction**   34
to the case studies and interviews
David Vernet and Leontine de Wit

04   **Merchandising for gatherers: interview with**   46
Oep Schilling and Vincent Sturkenboom, G-Star
David Vernet

05   **More than just architecture: interview with**   55
Eric Carlson, Louis Vuitton
David Vernet

Case studies   65

   Pfunds Molkerei, Dresden (1891)   66

   Kniže, Vienna (1905–13)   71

   Bally shoe shop, Paris (1928)   77

   Grayson, Seattle (1941)   82

   Olivetti showroom, New York (1954)   88

   Retti candle shop, Vienna (1965)   94

   Flos showroom, Milan (1968, 1976, 1984, 1990)   99

   MacLaren and Westwood, London (1971–80)   106

   Issey Miyake, Tokyo (1987)   110

   Comme des Garçons, New York (1988, 1998)   114
     and various locations (2004)

   10 Corso Como, Milan (1991)   122

   Mandarina Duck, Paris (2000)   128

   Oki-ni, London (2001)   134

   Camper Temporary Shop 'Walk in Progress',   138
     various locations (2000)

   Australian Homemade Ice Cream, Amsterdam (2002)   142

   Duchi shoe shop, Scheveningen (2004)   146

Annotated bibliography   150

Index   160

Illustration credits

Notes on contributors

Leontine de Wit is an architect/interior designer and Assistant Professor at the Chair of Architectural Design and Interiors (Faculty of Architecture, TU Delft). In 1998, she published a book on School–Housing flexible designs. She is currently researching the interdisciplinary relations between interior design and industrial design.

Sophie Dubuisson-Quellier is a Research Fellow in Sociology at the Centre de Sociologie des Organisations (CNRS, Sciences Po Paris). Her research interest is economic sociology and she has contributed to a specific approach to the functioning of markets, by analysing the role of the market mediation devices.

Mark Pimlott is an artist and designer. His public art works include 'Guinguette', Birmingham (2000), 'La scala', Aberystwyth (2003) and 'World', London (2002–10). His designs for interiors include Neckinger Mills, London (1988) and Red House, London (1999–present). He has taught architecture and visual arts since 1986, and is Professor in relation to practice in Interiors (Faculty of Architecture, TU Delft, 2002–05). His book *Without and Within* was published in 2006.

David Vernet is an architect and Assistant Professor at the Chair of Architectural Design and Interiors (Faculty of Architecture, TU Delft). He has been involved in teaching retail design and performance architecture.

Acknowledgements

The authors would like to thank Professor Tony Fretton, head of the Chair of Architectural Design and Interiors (Faculty of Architecture, TU Delft), for his support since the beginning of this project; their colleagues from the Chair of Architectural Design and Interiors, Christoph Grafe, Irene Cieraad, Jurjen Zeinstra and Udo Garritzmann for their comments and advice throughout this long process; Jan Paul Coelingh, for his commitment to achieving a clear and intelligible overview; Charlotte van Wijk and Hans Schouten for their help when it proved seriously needed; Marcelo Maquieira Piriz for his support and his input concerning the reality of contemporary shopping.

The contributors have been a tremendous source of inspiration and knowledge: Mark Pimlott, Sophie Dubuisson-Quellier, Eric Carlson, Oep Schilling and Vincent Sturkenboom have helped to cast a different light onto retail and to reveal its true implications.

Finally, the authors wish to gratefully acknowledge all the institutions and individuals who have given permission for their material to appear.

Foreword

Are boutiques, cafés, restaurants and bars the stuff of serious enquiry, and is what can be found in them of value to culture, architecture and architectural history? The series 'Interior Architecture', by the Chair of Interiors in TU Delft, of which this book is part, will show that the answer to both these questions is yes.

Architectural artifacts such as these are often financially and sensually extravagant, short-lived and rely as much on publicity as on their own physical form for their effect. They stylize cultural moments and deliver them through personal experience. These aspects make them significant as cultural phenomena.

Their ways of accommodating high design with the attitudes of commerce, clients and users and incorporating social and cultural rituals directly in their built fabric offer compelling lessons for architects who want to make buildings that are both high art and highly communicative.

In historical terms, they are among the places where the drama of making sense of the social, political and economic events that shape the modern world have been played out.

In shops and boutiques these deep events are manifested on the surface of society as fashion and reflected in design as style, and it might be said that this is the true subject of the book.

Mark Pimlott's introductory chapter, 'The boutique and the mass market', discusses the many other connections between those two levels while Sophie Dubuisson-Quellier in her chapter, 'The shop as market space', discusses the transactions before, during and after selling from her perspective as a Research Fellow at the Centre de Sociologie des Organisations, Paris.

In Chapters 4 and 5, David Vernet's interviews with the design departments of G-Star and Louis Vuitton show very lucidly the particular relationship between business and imagery that typifies fashion retailing and makes boutiques a compelling subject of study.

However, the heart of the book consists of David Vernet and Leontine de Wit's series of detailed case studies of boutiques that have shaped the genre. Though principally about boutiques for clothes and equipment – apparel for bodies and places – the case studies begin with a shop for the body itself, the Pfund dairy in Dresden from 1891. Here the strong ambition for social reform is manifested through diet, hygiene, social gathering and exposure to art. This design is not alone in having an explicit basis of ideas and values. All those studied turn out to be ideologically informed.

Kniže, the gentleman's clothing shop of 1905, is infused with Adolf Loos' theories of the relation of artifacts to culture and his sense of Vienna as a failing imperial capital from which a troubled modernism was flowing.

In contrast, Victor Gruen's configuration of shops for the US clothing chain Grayson of 1940, as boutiques infused with the techniques of suburban shopping, projects an optimistic view of

American consumer society and the development of the idea of consumers as individuals.

At the present time, Oki-ni in London of 2001 deals with the merger of traditional retailing with on-line selling. The design by 6a architects possesses the laconic quality, offhand styling and televisual view of the world that has accompanied the fluidity and uncertainty of recent times.

All the case studies in this book portray the development of retail architecture over one hundred years and indicate the future trends.

Tony Fretton
Professor, Chair of Interiors
Faculty of Architecture
Technical University of Delft
The Netherlands

The boutique and the mass market
Mark Pimlott

1.1 Prada Epicentre
(Rem Koolhaas, 2001)

1
M. Fogg, *Boutique: A 60s Cultural Phenomenon*, London: Mitchell Beazley, 2003

The boutique – the very word conjures up images of swinging London and the King's Road in the 1960s – was the humble descendant of two specific types of retail entities. The first, found in the arcades of the metropolitan centres of the nineteenth century, was the small shop with carefully crafted interiors purveying specialist commodities. The second was the appended *prêt-à-porter* concern of *haute couture* houses of the early twentieth century, offering well-designed accessories rather than *couture* at affordable prices.[1] The boutique of the 1960s shared characteristics of both: the idea of being special sprinkled upon customers by the nineteenth-century shop and the accessibility and entertainment provided by *au courant* design.

The boutique – that special enterprise, that little world unto itself, enticing customers to its interior, seducing them, offering them something exclusive and unique reflecting their proprietors and, by association, their own individuality – suffered from the twentieth century's particular elaboration of the condition of modernity. The devastation of the Great War (1914–18), the ensuing political uncertainty, global economic collapse and the catastrophe

1.2 GUM arcade in Moscow
(Alexander, Pomerantsev, 1893)

2
J.F. Geist, *Le Passage*, Liège, 1982

3
S. Buck-Morss, *The Dialectics of Seeing*, Cambridge, MA: MIT Press, 1989

of the Second World War (1939–45) all combined to cause the boutique's great home – the arcade – to fall into disuse and disrepute.[2] Retiring from its role as the abode of specialist and luxury commodities, the arcade (fig. 1.1) came to provide marginal shelters for businesses and goods that had departed from the scenes of urban consciousness. Walter Benjamin evoked this world of abandoned utopias and *kitsch* in the many notes that survive from his *Arcades Project*.[3] Thus exiled, small specialist shops were forced to survive in different contexts: in boulevards, high streets and, from the 1950s, in shopping malls: those quasi-public environments devised for everyone rather than *cognoscenti*; designed for generic conditions rather than specific *milieux*. The small shop was largely absent from the consumer psyche. Instead, the 'retail outlet' dominated high streets and malls, catering predominantly to a clientele of predictable circumstances with equally predictable spending habits. A mass market had come into being as a direct consequence of the Second World War. In the United States, government, industry, business and finance actively encouraged

4
Lisbeth Cohen, 'Is There an Urban History of Consumption?', *Journal of Urban History*, 1991

5
H. Sicherman, 'America and the West: Lessons from the Marshall Plan', Online. Available www.fpri.org/ww/0103.199801. sicherman.lessonsfromthe marshallplan.html

6
A. Forty, *Objects of Desire*, London: Thames and Hudson, 1986, p. 62

7
S. Stern, *The Marshall Plan: A German Point of View*, Online. Available www.germany. info/relaunch/culture/history/ marshall.html

Americans to consume on an epic scale, and provided the means to do so through the enablement of loans, mortgages and credit.[4] In Europe, the Marshall Plan (1947), directed at the post-war rebuilding of institutions and society, provided cash and the commodities upon which it could be spent, and so constructed another consumer society parallel to and dependent upon America's own.[5] The prevailing tendency in both situations was the production and consumption of a limited number of goods that were deemed to be essential: equipment for the home and for individual mobility. The demand for items was determined so as to be predictable, and integrated with industrialized production that had recently been dedicated to armaments.[6] It was only when these 'essential' desires had been substantially fulfilled that more particularized forms of consumption for a large public were able to re-emerge.

Such forms were not necessarily dedicated to so-called luxury goods, but to goods that would have been considered exclusive in the 1950s. Such a description held true for the small shops of the arcades. Particularity, that in some way reflected the specificity of the consumer's desires and the actual specificity of individuals and groups within society, was a quality that was 'rediscovered', developed and exploited. In the United States, this rediscovery was coincident with the rise of the civil rights movement, student movements and the visibility and realization of lifestyles other than those of the white, suburban middle class. By the mid-1960s, people increasingly regarded themselves as individuals or 'free agents' rather than as consumers with common aims, class or ethnicity. In Western Europe, the careful, transnational management of Marshall Plan funds[7] and the structuring of states along the broad principles of social welfare-tempered capitalism led to widespread consumer confidence, although this was experienced quite differently in each country.

The boutique's reappearance within fully developed consumer economies obliged it to relate to mass markets, regardless of its modesty or particularity to locale. This relation to markets or audiences was quite different from the business contexts characteristic of the specialist shops of the nineteenth and early twentieth centuries, and caused boutiques and their owners to find new ways of representing and situating themselves in order to retain their 'uniqueness'.

The boutique concept

In the mid-1960s, the boutique made its reappearance as a manifestation and in the service of a re-emergent individualism, the fruit of a newly adult bumper generation – the so-called 'Baby Boomers' – born immediately after 1945. The boutique found itself situated in the context of a highly-developed and competitive mass market. These two potentially conflicting realities came into focus at approximately the same time. The boutique had already been isolated as a particular phenomenon in British retailing: it was first noted in 1957 as a specialized fashion outlet contained within a department

8
Fogg, op. cit.

9
Fogg, op. cit.

10
Fogg, op. cit.

11
Fogg, op. cit.

12
Fogg, op. cit.

13
Books of Style: Uniforms for the Radical Set, New York Times, 8 June 2003, Online. Available http://query.nytimes.com/gst/full page.html?res=9C0DE5DC1639F9 3BA35755C0A9659C8B63&sec=& pagewanted=print

14
The Beatles' Apple Boutique, Online. Available www.strawberry walrus.com/applestore.html

store, selling ready-to-wear clothes by designers as opposed to the wholesale fashion that dominated the main store.[8] In advance of this format, Coco Chanel's Maison Couture contained a boutique selling accessories and perfume in 1929.[9] Designers such as Mary Quant took their small-scale, home-based productions into small shops, and offered clothes and accessories to young customers who wanted to express themselves through the purchase of inventive and non-conformist designs that were unavailable in the high street. In a moribund context, these products carried the aura of uniqueness. Customers identified with the boutiques' (and their owners'/designers') quite explicit ideas concerning ways of living, which were 'woven into' their products. In the case of Quant, Chanel and her ideas served as exemplars.[10] Customers were consumers of those ideas. The products of these boutiques in some way *represented* the interests and desires of their consumers. Shoppers often left the shops wearing their purchases, as though their visit to the boutique was part of their own personal transformation.[11]

The interiors of these boutiques reflected the particularity of their owners, and stood as expressions of those individuals' ethos. In many cases, the businesses of each of these proprietors had started in their homes.[12] Mary Quant felt that people expressed themselves in what they wore – as essentially joyous, sexually charged – and the interior of her boutiques were consequently 'fun'. The seduction therein was a promise of liberation. Zandra Rhodes's boutique was a place where people hung out to be part of a scene, so much so that the business end of its operation never quite came to fruition.[13] The Beatles had a boutique, Apple, which was simply a meeting place for people who wanted to be touched by their mystique, and to brush with celebrities. The sale of products was just one component of the package, not central to the Apple 'experiment' and probably the least successful.[14] Celebrity was an important aspect of the boutique concept: the boutique was an expression of individuality which people could touch and share (as opposed to a celebrity that people wanted to get a piece of), an ideal outlet for fan/consumer identification. Apple was representative; so was George Best's boutique. The boutique depended upon the personality of its proprietors, and accorded celebrity to them: Mary Quant, Barbara Hulanicki (Biba), Tommy Roberts (Mister Freedom); in the 1970s, Vivienne Westwood (SEX and others), Paul Smith. Expression and success in Britain were a relative novelty, and those who achieved it in various walks of life, through irreverence, wit and creativity were lionized by a young public looking to assume control of their world. The training these consumers received through advertising that consumption was the route to realization of desire made their identification with fashion designers and boutiques natural.

Celebrity was one aspect of the boutique's appeal, fitting in neatly with a full evolution of consumer culture, in which advertising enticed a completely 'new' generation, one that was furthermore

15
Imaginary Magnitude: The White Heat of Technology, Online. Available www.uefap.co.uk/listen/exercise/whiteheat/whiteheat.htm

16
Expo 67 Man and his World/Terre des Hommes: Official Guide/Guide Officiel, Montréal, 1967

17
Fogg, op. cit.

18
Sixties Central: Mary Quant, Online. Available www.geocities.com/FashionAvenue/Catwalk/1038/quant.html

19
History of Fashion Designer Mary Quant, Online. Available www.designerhistory.com/historyoffashion/quant.html

20
Mary Quant, Online. Available www.maryquant.co.uk

21
A.W. Turner, *The Biba Experience* (2004), Online. Available www.thebibaexperience.com/intro.html

fed on utopian promises and imagery. In America, this utopia was to be realized in the form of a 'Space Age', representing a new phase of technological revolution spearheaded by space exploration, computing and communications technology; in Britain, this was encapsulated by Prime Minister Harold Wilson in the phrase, the 'white heat' of technology.[15]

The prevailing rhetoric was that the world was to be liberated through technology (its incipient promise).[16] One aspect of that liberation was the very real freedom to consume, fuelled by credit. If there was to be a sense of liberation within this context, then variety or choice was the necessary correlate: the freedom to choose. It was implied, particularly in advertising, that it was possible to make a choice in lifestyle, or choose fragments of a variety of lifestyles that suited one's personality. Uniqueness was for everyone. With that came the freedom to define one's beliefs, ideological, religious or otherwise. Conflicts naturally arose with a variety of interesting consequences. These freedoms – complete with their contradictions – became fuel for designers, who freed themselves from adherence to conventional precedents: their work was characterized by spontaneity, impermanence and references to popular culture; they borrowed freely from outward signs of consumerism, sub-cultures and 'ethnic' sources, history and space-age futurism.

The material that designers referred to communicated to customers because it enveloped consumers and creators alike: framed within the outlets and language of mass communication, the portrayal of manifestations of popular culture suited their selling to a mass market. It was immediately evident to designers such as Mary Quant that the ideal relation to the consumer lay more in appeals to this market, to larger groups of people,[17] to a generation apparently moving in the same direction. The single Quant boutique, the unique experience related to Mary Quant's world-view – inspired by the simple and iconoclastic figure of Coco Chanel, who really invented the boutique in the modern form as a place to shop in the world of the designer in a relaxed manner[18] – was broadened so that there were several boutiques, not only in the same city, but in different parts of the country, in other cities, even in other countries, in entirely different markets.[19] The scale of operations of the company increased dramatically to simultaneously accommodate and stimulate demand. Quant's operation spread across London, then Britain, then America and beyond. It is currently owned by a Japanese concern and situated as a worldwide brand.[20] Barbara Hulanicki's Biba grew very quickly from one boutique to a department store in London's Kensington High Street with a mail order service.[21] Its offerings of Art Nouveau and Art Deco motifs – evoking the scenery and accoutrements of decadence – first in clothes and then in all sorts of products and goods for the home and the individual, represented the fantasy of the many rather than the few. (Biba's rapid expansion was faster than its ability to exploit its market, however, and it failed, ensuring its legendary status. It is currently undergoing a renaissance.) The simple napkins and tablecloths business of Laura Ashley quickly grew to sell simple fashions sold in a series of boutiques, then a large store in London selling household goods, a mail-order service and outlets in America and elsewhere.[22] It, too, is now owned by a Japanese concern.[23]

Boutique as device

The boutique as a 'one-off' phenomenon was legendary and relatively short-lived. Its success, as part of the blossoming of a particular period of culture in which change seemed possible and its manifestations abundant, ultimately relied upon the mechanisms of success – coincident with the mechanisms of fame – that were germane to its markets. This mass market required particular forms of address. The interior of the shop signified the boutique; its location in downtown and then regional shopping malls distributed it; advertising and promotion in mass-media outlets (particularly printed media) marketed it. As long as the retailer retained the aura of specificity to markets or audiences through its communications, its outlets would retain the aura of the boutique. The boutique, finally, was the outpost of the retailer's aura. The boutique signified uniqueness and represented its customers' – its consumers' – select judgement.

The pattern of growth – from garret-based production through high street boutique to presence in the mass marketplace through advertising and promotion – became the standard development from obscurity to prosperity for individual entrepreneurs. The various successes following this course were celebrated in the editorial pages and features of magazines, whose very existence depended upon advertising revenue. Boutique designers' products were frequently embedded in the economic life of department stores, making those retailers continuously relevant.[24] This real relationship – in the marketplace and in the structure of magazine publicity and finance – helped secure the position of 'small' designers in the mass market. The genius of retail entrepreneurs was in their ability to understand and command this mass market.[25] Once in the mass marketplace, the outposts of so-called smaller retailers could appear anywhere: in a high street, shopping mall or airport. They appeared wherever the market – by implication, their audience – wanted them to be. Because their outlets were discrete and modest (with designs apparently particular to each outlet), they were flexible, and could withdraw from financially difficult circumstances easily. They could appear, and disappear.

The market placement strategies of these designers' companies became useful, ultimately, to larger commercial concerns. Benetton, a company that began as a family operation, was able to operate at the scale of the department store on a national and international level in a short period of time, but acknowledged that its target audience (young, with moderate resources) responded to boutique-style

22
Laura Ashley Heritage, Online. Available www.lauraashley.com/ webapp/commerce/command/ ExecMacro/Laura_Ashley/macros/ about_us/index.d2w/report

23
Sixties Central: Biba, Online. Available www.geocities.com/ FashionAvenue/Catwalk/1038/ biba.html

24
Fogg, op. cit.

25
Fogg, op. cit.

facing page
1.2 Louis Vuitton in Paris: façade on Champs Elysées

07 The boutique and the mass market

26
Benetton: The Company's History, Online. Available www.museedela pub.org/pubgb/virt/mp/benetton/ index.html

environments.[26] Benetton recognized the boutique as a *motif* which could be distributed in as dense concentrations as could be sustained in any particular locale. The design of its boutiques was recognizable world-wide through the most minimal of devices: the shop signage, the modest modifications in colour and ironmongery to standard, mass-produced shop fronts and the colourful clothes within. The interiors were accumulations of off-the-shelf shop-fitting equipment, requiring only correct placement in relation to the consumer, something which had already been scientifically described.

Retail chains such as Benetton in Europe and The Gap in the United States catered to largely young audiences: they eventually acquired other brands that served markets both 'above' and 'below' their own target audience, and thus expanded their reach and established a tiered retailing strategy. In one direction, The Gap acquired the Banana Republic, a set of two shops in 1983, and situated the brand so to serve a 'discerning' consumer group;[27] in the other, it launched the company Old Navy, aimed at an audience dedicated to 'fun, fashion, and value' in 1994.[28] The company built a vertical or pyramidal target audience, in which each brand occupied a tier that related to and referred, or aspired to, the condition – income bracket, style, lifestyle – of that immediately above it. The Gap served a mass market in ever larger and more ubiquitous retail environments: its market strategy nevertheless appealed to those specialist retailers who saw the value of presence across vertical market groupings. The rampant successes tied to this strategy – wherein a company was assembled from 'a family' of brands targeted at various levels of the marketplace – led to this becoming standard practice in the acquisition atmosphere of business in the 1980s and 1990s.

27
About Gap, Inc., Online. Available www.gapinc.com/public/About/ about.shtml

28
About Gap, Inc.: Milestones, Online. Available www.gapinc.com/public/ About/abt_milestones.shtml

This was not lost on those luxury brands who had found that their markets had been eroded by the expanded reach of popular and 'boutique' brands. Traditionally, these luxury brands had been reliant upon their status, manifest in the exclusivity of their products, the sites of their appearance (events, editorial features, selective advertising, salons, the bodies of celebrities and royalty) and the rarity of their shops, another measure of their exclusivity. In danger of being rendered obsolete or left with very narrowly defined markets, a series of takeovers and mergers of luxury brands in the late 1980s and early 1990s established conglomerates or 'retail groups', incorporating all aspects of their particular, specialized markets. For example, the creation of LVMH (Louis Vuitton Moët Hennessy) in 1987 ensured that a large portion of expenditure in the retail area would find itself within the shelter of one corporate umbrella. This group covered the markets of 'wines and spirits; fashion and leather goods; perfumes and cosmetics; watches and jewellery; selective retailing; and other activities'.[29] LVMH furthermore recognized the necessity of broadening their appeal, and speculated that their exclusivity could be made accessible to a wider public through publicity and expressions of their environments, either mediated or actualized.

29
LVMH Group: Moët Hennessy Louis Vuitton: World Leader in Luxury, Listed on CAC 40 Index, Online. Available www.lvmh.com

The image of these brands was made more visible and intentionally more appealing or alluring to a mass public, conveyed through its traditional avenues of publicity (fig. 1.2); and through aggressive advertising, the expansion of the variety and nature of their products and the multiplication of their retail outlets. The critical and necessary aura of exclusivity of such brands – their unique selling point – was carried by the brands' identities rather than by the nature of the brands' products, environments or audiences. Luxury brands invaded the mass market and exploited its methods of organization and communication, assuming strategies that resembled those of mass-market merchandisers.

Icons and disguises

Advertising for these luxury brands – now either fronted by or massed together in large corporations – typically exploited the fantasy and plenitude associated with luxury and its surfaces. The complete artificiality offered by, for example, an advertisement for a Gucci bag, was precisely parallel to the experience a customer might anticipate in the enveloping, specific environment of a tiny, perfect shop. The resulting shops, no longer exclusive by their rarity, but rolled out in cities all over the world, reflected the atmosphere generated by their publicity and the expectations of their newly courted audiences: their surfaces assumed great importance. Their interiors of these very attractive *super-boutiques* owed much to ingenious lighting arrangements, highly polished material treatments (such as those devised by Tom Ford for Gucci; or by Jacques Helleu for Chanel) and iconic architectural containers: buildings that looked more like images than like buildings. Shops for Louis Vuitton by Jun Aoki or Kazuyo Sejima; and for Prada by Herzog and de Meuron were notable for their indebtedness to publicity's virtual surfaces and environments. These outlets could be qualified as *boutiques* in that they conveyed the precision of such places, and furthermore in that they represented the 'idea' of the brand as it had been nurtured within its audience through publicity. It is in the nature of publicity of luxury goods that the consumer is intended to identify with the uniqueness and exclusivity of the object of desire: it mirrors and represents the individuated consumer, who is obliged to suffer the paradox of feeling uniquely attracted to a mass-produced artefact subject to mass publicity.

In the Prada 'Epicenters', designed by Rem Koolhaas/OMA/AMO in New York, Los Angeles and San Francisco, a new kind of shop and set of relations between customer and retailer was envisaged. In their realization, the repeatability of luxury products was rendered transparent. The interior of the New York boutique – with its tribune for the display of shoes and special events, display cages ranging across the ceiling on tracks, cylindrical glass lift, billboard-scale photographic wallpaper, changing rooms with glass walls rendered opaque at the press of a pedal, and an information system that allowed workers and clients alike to have full descriptions of and access to the store's

30
Case Studies: Prada Introduction,
Online. Available www.ideo.com/
case_studies/prada.asp?x=1

31
Prada Info Systems Case Study,
Online. Available http://rfid.blue
starinc.com/resources/Zebra%20
Case%20Study-%20What%20
Retailers%20Can%20Learn.pdf

32
Prada Epicenter Revisited,
Online. Available www.freds
house.net/archive/000159.html

products – was intended to be a delivery mechanism for a full, abundantly available range of (admittedly desirable) products.[30] The critical component of the design, with which the architects were closely involved, was a computerized information system operated by staff and customers that showed the variety of products and their availability.[31] It was hoped that staff would be able to tailor their attention to the customers' desires and customize their shopping, and to communicate effectively with other staff while continuing to attend to them. Customers would thus be enabled to make choices as easily as possible. This, of course, was devised to increase the volume of sales, but also to engineer a shopping experience closer to that of online purchasing, with its sense of privacy, and streamlined selections based on the shopper's preferences, either stated or inferred by that individual's purchasing history. The 'customization' of the relationship between the retailer and the customer was precisely analogous to the experience of a small shop selling specialist goods to a known, individual customer: a *boutique*. The computer system was not, however, taken to by staff, or understood by customers,[32] and so the New York Prada store remained an interior closely associated with its publicity aura: reinforced by its architect's rhetorical advocacy and its own celebrity, augmented by its appearance as a protagonist on television's *Sex and the City*.

Raised to the status of celebrity (like Macy's and Tiffany's before it), Prada's New York 'boutique' appeared in the manner that specialist commodities had been appearing for some time: as a token. In film, luxury commodities served as promotional devices, at once signifying themselves and conferring 'glamour' upon the scenes of their appearance. In music videos broadcast on MTV or other outlets, they were appropriated, by rap artists in particular, precisely for their connotations of elevated status and wealth. In this context, the artifacts (luxury automobiles, accessories, drinks) acted as totems: their purported significance was used to transform audience associations into tribal identification. The location of such products in mediated scenes – *simulacra* of the popular realm – in which they were designed to play symbolic roles, lent them notoriety, enhancing their aura and their apparent involvement in 'real life', consequently extending their markets.

Luxury brands diversified their production to accommodate and infiltrate these new potential markets: motifs drawn from street culture, such as 'bling' (the 'sound' of light reflecting off jewellery) and graffiti, were used to cultivate different, wider audiences. There was a correlate: these new products lent street credibility to its traditional customers. This retail strategy had been used previously by luxury brands and boutique owners in the 1980s and 1990s, in those designs for shop interiors and advertisements that adopted the tropes of the contemporary art and its sites. Appropriation of the 'white cube' and 'documentary photography' – for example, by Helmut Lang (owned by Prada) – associated products and producers with 'high' culture *of the*

1.3 Vuitton in Paris:
interior detail

moment, and blurred their activities and appearances with those of art and design.

For corporate retail concerns, a path opened for both actual and mediated retailing environments that sought legitimacy through association with other manifestations of culture, so-called 'low' culture, particularly photography, publicity and 'the street'. Such environments blurred differences between these manifestations, denied their specificity and used them either as props or *décor*, in inverse to film and rap's uses of luxury brands as symbols. The movement toward equivalence in products and their representations – both 'high' and 'low' – had been characteristic of the relationship between advertising, fashion and popular culture in the 1960s, and integral to the boutique's re-emergence.[33] At that time, boutiques borrowed from the techniques of large retailers and publicity to forge relationships with the mass market. By its nature, the movement to equivalence offered each type of producer the possibility to act in the realm and in the manner of another: within this expanded field, associations with and allusions to other producers and to other forms and tropes of production have maximized the perception of the market, its apparent scope (wherein 'high' and 'low' are equivalent and thus connected) and the potential for making money.

In this atmosphere of one world (brought together by publicity), retailers have been enabled to evince qualities – classically germane to

33
Mark Pimlott, 'Architecture and
the Condition of Publicity', *NAi
bulletin*, Rotterdam, 2006

11 The boutique and the mass market

34
'LVMH Group: Moët Hennessy Louis Vuitton: World Leader in Luxury, Listed on CAC 40 Index', op. cit.

35
V. Friedman, 'Can Art Ever Sell Handbags?', *Financial Times/How to Spend It*, no. 152, December 2005, p. 6–8

36
Fondazione Prada, Online. Available www.fondazioneprada.org

37
Galerie du jour agnès b., Online. Available www.galeriedujour.com/gdj/exposition

38
agnès b. Online Store, Online. Available www.shoponlineusa.agnesb.net/about.cfm

39
Moss, Online. Available www.mossonline.com

the boutique – of eccentricity, uniqueness and philanthropy. In the case of large retail companies, LVMH pursues a policy of involvement with the arts:[34] Louis Vuitton's new store in Paris contains large-scale, permanent installations by artists whose ostensible purpose is to make its customers think about or be in culture while shopping.[35] The presence of art, treated seriously and at considerable expense by its hosts, lends a different order of credibility to the company, in which it becomes patron, and 'not just a retailer' (fig. 1.3). The corporation thus acquires a more human character, appealing to its customers as human and thoughtful, and transferring these qualities to its customers through the silent contract that exists between them. Miuccia Prada owns a contemporary art foundation,[36] whose activities, although separate from those of Prada's fashion stores, invites confusion in distinctions between the programmes and thus the purposes of Prada as a whole, making that global retail enterprise appear to operate following the idiosyncratic policies of the proprietor, and hence, of a boutique. Agnès Trouble, the proprietor of agnès b., runs art and publishing programmes alongside the retail operations of agnès b. stores, which lend the impression of an intimate and individual nature to what is a global retail concern.[37] One of its own websites associates this individual touch with the individual expression of the customer:

> For over 25 years now, wearing agnès b. has become akin to the expression of one's character. As a designer, agnès still has time for her other passions as a photographer, film producer and an avid collector as well as a supporter of the arts.[38]

These latter two companies are indeed the fruit of concepts of their proprietors, and with evident success have situated the intimacy of the boutique idea within the realities of the mass market.

The boutique appropriates the boutique

In the atmosphere of appropriation, interference and transgression fully cultivated by the turn of the twenty-first century, one might conclude that the boutique has been able to recuperate its own characteristics in the wake of its appropriation by luxury retailers, to appear, again, as unique. The boutique is a captivating model, evidently capable of conveying its ideas at the scale of either global operation, single retail outlet, or website. A number of examples of retail operations at different scales serve to illustrate the lasting viability and appeal of the boutique motif.

A boutique in this mould is the New York design store Moss,[39] resembling a fashion shop, wholesale warehouse, *Wunderkammer* and museum all at once, rendering everything inside, no matter how different or unique, equivalent. Its sampling of artifacts is eclectic, bound together by the fetishism of an unidentified 'collector' that is the store and its implied proprietor. The shop is an exhibition of good taste, captive of neither time nor ideology. This quality is passed onto

the customer, who is posited as a fellow *aficionado* or *connoisseur*. The delectability of the objects on display naturally charge that connoisseur with the role of consumer, who browses the extremely diverse contents with very much the manner of a private individual browsing a website that somehow accommodates his/her catholic, yet discerning, tastes.

The eclecticism and extreme individualism proposed by Moss are echoed in its own website, wherein each artefact is displayed on a white field like some piece of candy, there for the private enjoyment of the viewer. This quality is pursued by retail entities that have no actual street presence whatsoever: the Internet *prêt-à-porter* fashion retailers Yoox[40] and net-à-porter (.com)[41] present themselves on their webpages as interfaces, evoking both fashion magazine and boutique, offering shoppers the possibility to browse and to examine articles closely, at different angles and in detail. The graphics of the webpages are redolent of those of glossy magazine spreads. The process of purchase is simple, quick and not intruded upon by either sales assistants or loud music. Items are delivered to the customer's home address in carefully designed packaging (of the brand that one has purchased), in the manner of the boutique: the customer is apparently treated like an individual who wants to be treated like an individual.

The aura of privacy and personal, individual (and eclectic) taste cultivated by the Internet is used by the London shop of Oki-ni, which appears as an actualized extension of its own Internet site.[42] Its

40
Welcome to Yoox: The Never-Ending Store, Online. Available www.yoox.com

41
Net-à-porter: The World's First Global Fashion Boutique, Online. Available www.net-a-porter.com/cgi-bin/NETAPORTER.storefront

42
Oki-ni, Online. Available www.oki-ni.com

1.5 Guerrilla store in Berlin

43
Fogg, op. cit.

44
Vivienne Westwood, Online.
Available www.viviennewestwood.
com/flash.php

45
*Comme des Garçons Guerrilla Store
– Berlin, Hong Kong, Singapore,
Cologne, Reykjavik, Athens*, Online.
Available www.guerilla-store.com/
flash.php

extreme ambiguity – its *un-shop-ness* – seems to point to another direction for the boutique, one in which the boutique is a transient presence with no visible proprietor, and the consumer is entirely responsible for the fulfilment of his/her desire.

The quality of fleeting presence, particular to the boutique of the 1960s and 1970s[43] gave the consumer the feeling of being special, a connoisseur of those things that are of the moment, that come and go, and define the time one lives in, through a private perspective. Treasured shops would appear, then (usually due to financial inviability) disappear, or reappear in another guise, with another name. The 1970s boutiques of Vivienne Westwood and Malcolm MacLaren in London's King's Road, such as SEX and World's End[44] employed this tenuousness as a strategy, proposing a method of attack and withdrawal, camouflage and outrage, that was specific to the nature of the boutique and central to their whole enterprise (fig. 1.4). As an echo of that *modus operandi*, Rei Kawakubo's Comme des Garçons is currently establishing – and rapidly dismantling – a series of shops called 'Guerilla stores' in cities across the world that are devised to exist for only a few months, occupying existing premises as they are found.[45] The stores appear as special presences to *cognoscenti*, and then close, taking their merchandise away from the addresses (announced on the Internet) which appear to be untouched once they depart, hence enhancing the stores' status as events (fig. 1.5). These events are completely public, known internationally, yet they are designed to appeal to the individual's – the consumer's – sense of private discovery.

The project of the boutique, even that conceived by Coco Chanel, has always maintained the idea of engaging a mass market in a fantasy of individual adventure. This principle has seen violent development and modification because of the very nature of the mass market and capital. Retail concerns have become, by necessity, international operations. These retailers' skills in making their operations continuously relevant and captivating have required constant re-propositions of form, content and relations. Their strategies, and the boutique itself, will undoubtedly continue to develop in accordance with the extreme demands of the market and its innate antagonism, between individuality and conformity.

**The shop as market space
The commercial qualities of retail
architecture
Sophie Dubuisson-Quellier**

2.1 Kniže salon

1
D. Miller, *A Theory of Shopping*, 1998, Ithaca, NY:
Cornell University Press, p. 5; A. Warde, *Consump-
tion, Food and Taste*, London: Sage, 1997, p. 196

2
P. Steiner, *La sociologie économique*, Paris: La
découverte, Repères, 2005, p. 35; F. Cochoy and
S. Dubuisson-Quellier, 'Les professionnels du
marché: vers une sociologie du travail marchand',
Sociologie du travail, 3(42), 2000; M. Callon, *The Laws
of the Market*, Oxford: Blackwell, 1998, p. 15

3
S. Barey, F. Cochoy and S. Dubuisson-Quellier,
'Designer, packager, merchandiser. Trois
professionnels pour une même scène marchande',
Sociologie du travail, 3(42), 2000

The social sciences have shown an interest in consumption patterns, purchasing practices and consumer behaviour, but they have tended to overlook the subject of commercial space or architecture.[1] Nevertheless, a number of recent works have sought to understand the functioning of markets by returning to fundamental notions of commercial exchange.[2] This type of sociology is principally concerned with the functioning of market intermediation such as brand, advertising, merchandising, product design and packaging.[3] One of the central tenets of this chapter is to demonstrate that retail architecture, too, is a vital mechanism in the functioning of market intermediation.

Retail architecture is defined as those market spaces, both real and virtual, that affect the relationship between supply and demand.[4]

4
F. Cochoy, 'L'hypermarché: jardin d'un autre type aux portes des villes', *Ethnologie française*, 35(1), 2005: 81–91; Th. Debril and S. Dubuisson-Quellier, '"Marée", "charcuterie-traiteur", "Le rayon traditionnel en grande surface"', *Ethnologie française*, 35(1), 2005: 93–102; F. Cochoy, and C. Grandclément, 'Publicizing Goldilocks' Choice at the Supermarket: The Political Work of Product Packaging, Shopping Carts, and Shopping Talk', in B. Latour and P. Weibel (eds) *Making Things Public: Atmospheres of Democracy*, 2005, Cambridge, MA: MIT Press; C. Licoppe, 'Faire ses courses par téléphone, faire ses courses par Internet: médiations technologiques, formes des échanges, de la relation commerciale et de la consommation', *Réseaux*, 106, 2001: 75–100

5
S. Barrey, *Le travail marchand dans la grande distribution alimentaire. La définition des relations marchandes*, PhD dissertation, Université Toulouse II, 2004

6
G. Simmel, *Philosophie de l'argent*, Paris: PUF, 1987, p. 49

The manifestation of this relationship between suppliers and demanders, sellers and buyers, will hereafter be referred to as the market relationship. Large retailers like supermarkets lend themselves more easily to spatial analyses of the market relationship than do other retail spaces, mainly because they serve to concentrate and amplify market intermediation forces.[5] Yet there is much to be learned from studying smaller retail spaces as well, namely the boutique or shop. Before returning to this theme of public and private retail space, an analysis of the shop will be presented that focuses on its status as a market space, and on its function as a mechanism for market intermediation.

Staging the market relationship

The following section will highlight the contribution of the shop to the construction of the market relationship. In Western culture, the influence of an anthropological vision of the commercial exchange is important. It has been thought of in terms of relationship between isolated buyers and sellers who have nothing in common besides the transaction being undertaken by them. In addition, the value of the products involved in the transaction is usually based upon a principle of commensurability.[6] The consumer is therefore said to engage in a series of calculations that equate value with price when choosing a product from what is on offer. One of the shop's goals is to invoke these principles of isolation, of separate identity between buyer and seller, and to provide the former with the opportunity to identify, classify, distinguish and otherwise appraise the products for sale. This separation was also a means to establish a warm relationship based on loyalty from both sides, as was the case in the old-fashioned retail relationship.

In the consumption process, buyer and seller are no more than ephemeral positions in a transaction. Present relationship is not considered warm and friendly but as purely commercial in nature, and therefore more businesslike and distant. Historically, the role of retail architecture was to ease the businesslike relation, mollifying the brutal and violent process of property exchange with rules of exchange (such as credits and postponed payments in the old-fashioned boutiques) and social rules (such as courtesy and reception). For this reason, some retail spaces today can exaggerate friendliness and warmth, for instance, by making their entryways extra large to convey a sense of welcoming openness, or integrating meeting spaces such as cafés or restaurants into their shops. But these kinds of architectural arrangements typify a preferred relation as well as the kind of customers it want to address. For example, a budget supermarket will radiate its cheapness by extra cold and harsh lighting, since a warm and friendly atmosphere in a shop demonstrates a kind and service-prone relationship, hence one that is more expensive.

If the history of retail is also a history of class, for shops for the upper class did not welcome everybody, today these class distinctions

7
M. Miller, *The Bon Marché: Bourgeois Culture and the Department Store, 1869–1920*, Princeton, NJ: Princeton University Press, 1994, p. 10

are no longer so clear. In Vienna, the shop Kniže, whose chairs and small salons continue the architectural arrangements of the late nineteenth century, is both inviting and exclusive, such as in the closed shops – *maisons* – where one had to ring the bell to be admitted or even had to make an appointment. The department store (figs 2.2, 2.3, 2.4), with its provenance in the opening of Paris's famous Bon Marché in 1852, was also designed with social class in mind.[7] This model was based on the sale of inexpensive products that were newly available thanks to the economies of scale realized by industrialization and mass production. Stores like Bon Marché opened up a whole new world of retail for the middle classes, one in which goods were affordable and constantly changing, allowing this social class, especially women, to reach new levels of consumption desires. They attracted their clientele by using three key principles: variety, novelty and service. For the first time, the middle class experienced shopping as an amusement, one that permitted them to benefit from services, such as doormen and porters, that once were reserved solely for the elite. Finally, the architecture of the first department stores evoked the modern and the monumental with abundant use of windows and metallic structures. Gustave Eiffel himself was involved in the original design conception of Bon Marché, which was meant to be luminous and immense, the better to show off the plethora of goods for sale. Some luxury boutiques reacted to the phenomenon of the department store by becoming (or like Kniže remaining) even more exclusive. Their definition of luxury was quasi-aristocratic and totally personalized. Their customers, ensconced in an intimate salon reserved exclusively, albeit temporarily, just for them, were pampered from the moment they set foot in the door. Nevertheless, department stores also proposed small salons dedicated to ladies rather than men (fig. 2.1).

Today, the staging of the market relationship can follow these classic formulas, or it can attempt to subvert them. This choice signifies that the same question – how to stage the market relationship – can be treated through myriad architectural means. These run the gamut between two poles, one in which the message or subject is made glaringly plain, the other in which it is voluntarily masked or effaced altogether. In terms of the former, architecture may highlight the cold and sometimes businesslike nature of the market relationship. Here one might see decoration that is brutally sparse and without frills, products that seem wrenched from the world that produced them, and a general ambience made devoid of warmth by crude lighting and excessive use of windows and glass. The shop is supposed to moderate the harshness of the market relationship; wrapping in effect lets the harshness out of the box while containing it within the box that is the shop itself. At the other architectural pole, the warmth of the social relationship is infused into the shop space with decoration that accentuates small, comfortable spaces and overall cosiness. It is in these spaces that social norms come into play most

2.2 Le Printemps, department store in Paris (architect, Sédille, 1881)

forcefully, for the architect must consciously choose which norms to signify in the 'comfortable' space, and which to subvert. Put another way, the staging of the market relationship today is less about making certain social distinctions apparent than about playing with established social codes that customers can identify. In this way, architecture can directly illustrate in the boutiques some of the social significations of the retail relationship: its brutality as well as its warmth, its social class

19 The shop as market space

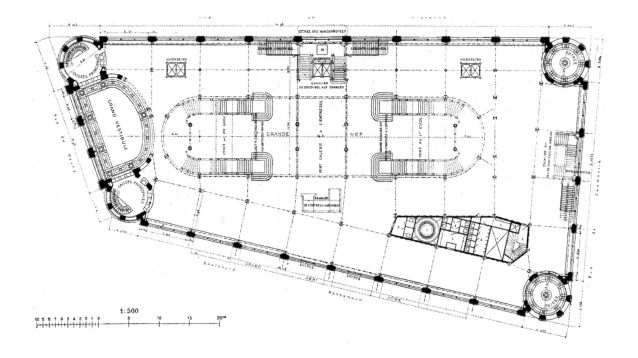

1:500

organization as well as its social class mixing, its contribution to the general production and consumption process as well as its capacity to provide non-standard products.

The changing roles of customers and staff

Retail architecture is the spatial expression of the envisioned relationship between customers and shop staff. For example, distinct spaces for customers and staff are manifestations of their different roles in the market mediation. Delineation of such spaces has traditionally been achieved through counters, service windows, front and back offices or by doors, partitions and curtains that indicate to the customer the areas to which he or she may have access. The historic development of this kind of architecture could be found in transgressive spaces that seek to blur or confuse the spatial boundaries between buyers and customers. In such spaces customers may enter areas normally closed to them, even ones that are clearly those of the seller. These kinds of retail designs also aim to remove some of the staff obligations, such as helping the customer make his choice, going to seek products for him, helping him try them on. Buyers and customers are exchanging roles since customers have to make their own choices and shop staff may refer to their own customer experience to help clients.

The aforementioned architectural details and their configuration not only separate space, they can also prescribe roles. For example, the wall-mounted sets of drawers behind the counter in the Kniže shop

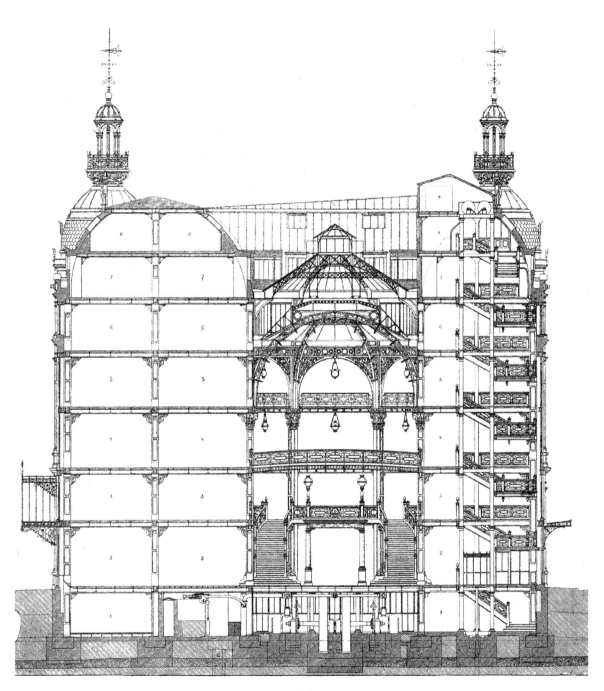

1:250

2.4 Le Printemps, section

21 The shop as market space

indicate that access to the products within is the prerogative of the shop staff and not the customers. The arrangement of furnishings in this way does more than dictate modes of perception and access by the customer; it also turns the seller into an indispensable intermediary in the transaction. In the traditional role-play of assisted sales situations, it is assumed that only the staff have qualified product knowledge. Customers are required to rely upon the salesperson in order to select a suitable product, and/or to handle that product in the correct way.

The advent of self-service, by contrast, marked a redistribution of retail space and action. More than just another selling technique, it revolutionized the traditional role-play, and gave the customer more agency.[8] Self-service practices emerged throughout the retail sector after the Second World War, usually in boutiques that sold products requiring the minimum of assistance. The packaging industry in the case of the supermarket predated the advent of self-service. Product information on packages or fixed quantities replaced the shop assistant. Also the introduction of labels with product information and washing instructions attached to textiles and clothing made the informed shop assistant more or less redundant. The primary advantage of self-service was lower prices, for it allowed shops to hire fewer personnel, thereby cutting costs. While this may have been the ideal case, this sales technique was not an easy one to implement. Managers found that they had to use gimmicks to attract wary customers, such as hiring actors to move through the store and demonstrate how simple this kind of shopping could be. Ultimately, customer resistance to self-service came from the fact that it required them to develop new competences in exchange for lower prices. It entailed a change of roles, for they had to learn not only how to become informed, or become customers who are capable of making decisions independently, but also how to be price-conscious customers who know what they want and where to look for it, who know how to compare products, and who are disciplined enough to pay for their shopping before leaving the shop.

Revised spatial organization

The customers' role change had profound implications for the spatial organization of the shop. The customer's path through the boutique had to be carefully anticipated and planned: shelves had to be accessible and products needed to be grouped together. The consumer competences were guided by in-store devices such as aisles, shelves and signs, which facilitate not only the identification of individual products, but also the comparison of products. Categorization and comparison form the foundation of economic intermediation, and they are what shops of all kinds strive to elicit from their customers – albeit in many different ways. In a grocery store, for example, products like coffee, filters, cereals and biscuits may be grouped in the 'breakfast section', thereby giving a coded

8
P. Du Gay, 'Self-Service: Retail, Shopping and Personhood', *Consumption, Markets and Culture*, 7(2), 2004: 149–63

2.5 Flos showroom in Milan, 1968

indication of appropriate product pairings or complements. Or, in Kniže, products might be grouped according to article of clothing, while in another shop they might be grouped by ensemble. Shops are, in essence, three-dimensional catalogues, places where products can be seen in ways that highlight their differences, as well as their similarities and complements. The department store's departments, the supermarket's aisles and the shop's salons are all spatial modalities that serve to classify, be it by type, colour, style or purpose. For example, in the Flos boutique, lights are presented according to their luminous effects or their shape (fig. 2.5). The products on offer are therefore only ever laid out in spaces that serve simultaneously to separate and segment them.

23 The shop as market space

Such thinking was the precursor to the fixed routing of shoppers, of which Ikea is a classic example. Ikea's customers are routed through the boutique in spiral fashion in order to expose them to as many products as possible, a device borrowed from museums that is now commonplace in every store of the brand. The persistence of this kind of retail architecture indicates that customers have become disciplined by following fixed routings, while at the same time they have gained the ability to circulate autonomously through a space. Today, in most boutiques, there is no explicit routing and it is not entirely self-service either. The shop assistant is still very important, if only because not all available products/models/varieties are on show. There is a counter or information desk. In contrast to the traditional shop, however, there is less pressure to buy. 'Just looking' has become a legitimate reason to enter a boutique.

The introduction of self-service by retailers was accompanied by the development of customer competencies in selection processes, which were now guided largely by in-store devices such as aisles, shelves and signs in supermarkets. The planned presentation of products was intended to facilitate the expression of choice, not merely display the full range of what was on offer. This kind of economic intermediation functions in two different ways. On the one hand, it must categorize the products according to what they have in common and, on the other, it must permit each product and its properties to be individually discerned by the customer so that they can be compared.

Intermediation can and should be thought of as one of the principal operations behind the market relationship. The Grayson shop reminds us that retail spaces, above all else, contain elements that prescribe action. At Grayson, customers circulate freely and have visual and physical access to all the products for sale, but most importantly they decide whether or not they want assistance in making their decisions. Grayson is an excellent example of a shop in which presentation is an art in itself. The shop's theatrical interiors, light-filled and open, are so attractive that the space alone brings people in the door. The idea of attracting shoppers with a splendid, or even an exotic interior including additional amusement was a marketing instrument already used in the late nineteenth-century department store, which really came of age in the 1950s in the United States and the 1960s in Europe with the birth of the shopping mall. The challenge for Grayson, and for all boutiques using this strategy, lies in making the otherwise sublime experience of shoppers into one that incites them to make purchases.

Finally, transactions would not be complete were the products not to change hands through payment operations, and these are also the object of various architectural treatments. The act of payment can be separated from the processes of choice and exchange such that the merchant, who is usually well in control of this stage of the commercial relationship, may choose to repress the idea for as long as possible. The position of cash registers in shops is therefore the result of a careful balance. Unlike in large stores, where the registers often appear in prominent and quasi-industrial fashion, shop owners walk a line between hiding or detaching them from the operations involving choice, and reminding or associating them with those operations.

The status of payment operations has evolved along with the retail industry. For example, in their quest to cut costs, chain stores began eliminating, as early as the late nineteenth century, the delivery and credit services that had to that point been included in the retail price. In shops, now that customers had to pay cash, the gleaming cash register took a conspicuous place to remind them of this new necessity. Later, with the development of self-service, the act of passing by the cash register became all that was left of the face-to-face contact between the customer and the salespeople. Payment was the final step in the path followed by customers through the store, as reflected by the positioning of cash registers just before the exit. Today, virtually anything is possible regarding the rules for this discrete but requisite operation. For example, certain butcher shops wish to revive the old image of the former neighbourhood establishment. In these shops the entire transaction, from butcher block to cash register, is handled by the owner. The fact that the presence of the shop owner is so noteworthy is a reminder of just how tenuous the link between owner and customer has become in contemporary retailing.

Retail space, however, is not only a location in which a type of social relationship is expressed, it is also a stage on which exchanges play out that are, for the most part, crafted elsewhere.

The shop as market intermediation device

Since the advent of self-service, shops also play a role in constructing market linkages. The market must not be seen as the fortuitous meeting of a pre-determined supply with an autonomously generated demand. Rather, it should be viewed as the result of market techniques and mechanisms that perpetually adjust supply to demand and demand to supply. Although retail architecture is an important market mechanism, the shop is much more than a mere supplement to marketing, advertising and/or packaging. It is, in effect, a space in which various market intermediation devices that were conceived of elsewhere are articulated. These devices are conceived of not by the shop owner or the shop's architect, but by manufacturers who engage in their own product positioning and marketing strategies. The place of sale is, after all, one of the fundamental components of the marketing mix concept. However, it is a mistake to view the shop as a simple theatre of marketing strategy because it also constitutes the primary link between the manufacturer and buyer. The shop is clearly a space in which a supply of products is concretely assembled and presented, and in which local demand is expressed. In this sense, the shop has a very specific role to play in market mediation. In order to examine more closely what that is, a tripartite concept of market function will be introduced. The first dimension will involve an assessment of the market, describing the ways by which market actors can define the demand side. The second will deal with how customers are attracted and kept, or on client recruitment and fidelity strategies. The final dimension will treat adjustment between supply and demand, describing the work by which market actors instil demand properties into a given supply of goods.

Representing the market

The work of constructing a representation of the market is in general something done between the factory and the point of sale. A shop that is a branch of a brand retailer, like the shoe company Camper, for example, will rely upon headquarters for market studies. It will also make those market studies possible by monitoring the social interactions that occur in the store and by contributing to the generation of customer and market data. In this sense, retail architecture can be thought of as something that gives sellers the opportunity to know more about their clients. Through combinations of dedicated space and technology, certain architectural settings can help them listen to the customers, deal with their complaints, and compile information about their profiles and habits. For example, private spaces lead customers to take their time and communicate their likes and dislikes to salespeople. The electronic tracking of customer purchases allows the seller to use payment procedures and the space allotted to them as areas of exchange for customer preferences. And, finally, spaces dedicated to pre-purchase activities like product trials are also ways of getting to know the customer.

An example of the latter can be found in record boutiques that allow customers to listen to songs before purchase. This service is valuable to customers and it gives the shop information about trends in the music market or customer reaction to certain songs or artists. These listening areas, which in some instances take up half the store, may be seen not as an extension of the boutique itself, but as its true centre. In contrast to this is the company Oki-ni, an online retailer that operates a small number of shops. These 'brick and mortar' spaces function more as show rooms than as retail outlets, since they have virtually nothing for sale in them. Oki-ni gauges customer reaction to what is on display not through customer feedback at its shops, but through the orders they place on its website after visiting the shop. New technologies have greatly expanded the realm of what is possible in this area, mainly by allowing for the rapid production of customer data that can be used during the sales interaction (fig. 2.6). The Prada store in New York, for example, has a way of electronically identifying consumers when they enter. Upon entry, customers are directed to those products that best suit their tastes, again with the aid of an electronic device.

Occasionally, the shop space itself is used as a tool for constructing market identity. The Parisian shop Colette or its Milanese counterpart 10 Corso Como are good examples of this phenomenon,

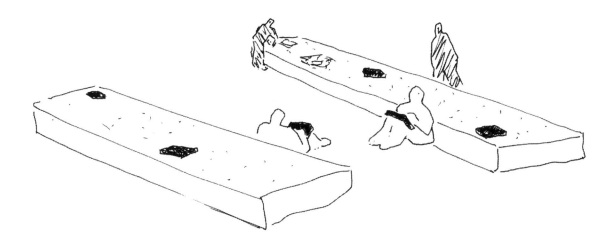

2.6 Oki-ni: the environment allows customers to browse the brand's website

with their super-trendy and mostly limited edition wares arranged, as if to underscore their rarity, in a museum-like setting. The space helps to create a particular rapport between the customer and the shop because those who buy are partaking directly in the lifestyle aesthetic proposed therein. The space itself segments the visitors, quickly capturing those who want to be in step with what is on offer. The shoe boutique Duchi is also in the business of identifying that niche of the market in which its potential devotees reside. Many of those who visit its store do so not necessarily to buy shoes, but rather to experience the carefully constructed atmosphere. By drawing people in with a certain kind of music, space and overall image, Duchi brings together the group of consumers that it wants as a client base. Both Duchi and Colette demonstrate well that the shop space can do more than just welcome customers whose characteristics have been pre-determined by the marketing strategies of manufacturers. They show that shops can themselves bring together groups of people that are likely to be consumers of the products on offer.

Customer recruitment and loyalty

Customer recruitment and fidelity activities normally occur between the boutique itself and through various advertising media channels that compete to capture customers.[9] The shop is of interest here because it constitutes a static recruitment mechanism, one that draws customers in from the public space outside using its exterior. This concept, first developed by large retailers, is more difficult to carry out in the city because the extent to which stores can recruit in this way is limited by the shop itself and by the surrounding businesses. Shop signs and windows are designed to function in such a way that the passer-by notices the shop, sees what is in the windows, and eventually crosses the threshold. In this sense, the shop is not just a reflection of the brand, but an autonomous mechanism that can acquire customers

9
L. McFall, 'The Language of the Walls: Putting Promotional Saturation in Historical Context', *Consumption, Markets and Culture*, 7(2), 2004: 107–28; F. Cochoy (ed.) *La captation des publics*, Toulouse: Presses universitaires du Mirail, 2004, p. 13

on its own. The Bally shoe shop is a good example of this. Despite the minimalist look of its storefront, the shop effectively attracts the attention of the passer-by by physically encroaching on the sidewalk. In addition to being imposing, this exterior invitation to enter can sometimes be intentionally ambiguous, as in the case of the shop Retti. There, the difficult entryway is intriguing, actually arousing curiosity in the passer-by (fig. 2.7).

Shop windows merit a veritable ethnography all on their own, given how much they have contributed to the construction of the market relationship. In 1830, when the first large retailers developed in northern Europe, they adopted the rule of 'small profit and quick return'[10] which allowed them to sell goods cheaply to customers who paid cash. Ultimately, as those from whom goods were bought became less and less like artisans and more like salespeople, set prices were affixed to products and credit sales and haggling were mostly eliminated. The price tag, but also the shop window, the initial function of which was to increase customers' confidence in retailing practices, thus took their place as methods of acquiring a clientele that would henceforth be part of a redefined relationship, that of 'no abatement and no second price', to use the terms of the day.

By the time it has fulfilled its recruitment function, the shop window has also created a relationship between the product and the customer. The windows present sketches or suggestions on how the materials on display can be combined based upon their similarities or differences. Once over the threshold, customers continue to be 'lured' through the shop at the suggestion of the architecture, the organization of space and the arrangement of furnishings. There is more to recruitment, however, than just the initial capturing of customers' attention: their loyalty must also be cultivated. Indeed, successful retailing has long been based upon the dual requirement that boutiques find new ways of attracting customers and new ways of keeping those already acquired. Changing what is for sale, or sometimes simply changing its presentation, are both means of inciting customers to return regularly. Here, the recruitment of customers and the generation of customer loyalty are part of the same operation.

In general, when it comes to loyalty, large retailers must win over customers by means other than the personal relationship between shop owner and customer used in traditional commerce. Bon Marché used to invite its customer to return again and again by making sure that there was always something 'just in' to see for the first time. And today, retailers have never turned over collections faster. Some shops have based their customer fidelity strategy on a system in which the products for sale have a limited shelf life that requires them to be continually and completely replaced with new products, so the customer must regularly come back to the boutique. The periodic introduction of the new products is an 'event' that draws customers back. Other shops, that are organized as show rooms, or that make

10
D. Davis, *A History of Shopping*, London: Routledge, 1966, p. 29

2.7 Retti: façade

use of stages, scenes or performances, are also using events to attract new customers and to draw back existing ones.

In the opposite approach, some stores recruit clients and generate loyalty by maintaining a constant standard, as was the case in the 1850s in Great Britain with certain grocery stores. This allows them to attract clients from beyond the immediate vicinity of the shop because patrons who have become accustomed to the standard will go to some

29 The shop as market space

lengths to find it. Thus, there are two approaches to recruitment and fidelity, one involving routine, the other novelty. In the former, customers return again and again to find what is familiar and unchanging, while in the latter they return to be surprised by shops that are never the same.

In addition to the curiosity mentioned earlier, architecture can also affect would-be customers with a specific aesthetic, or simply by catching the eye of those casually strolling by. Doing so is not a negligible task, but beyond getting customers in the door, these devices also highlight the ability of the shop to assert itself as a place or location. Camper, for example, allows its franchisees to open provisional, pre-fabricated stores next to locations where a new Camper boutique is in the process of being built. The idea is to create an event around the building of the new shop, and an occasion, albeit a temporary one, for selling shoes. This location next to a location is designed to mark the space where certain goods will be sold, to communicate to potential and future consumers what will be for sale. Just as stores in the nineteenth century used criers to attract customers by announcing promotions or the arrival of new merchandise, so Camper uses its provisional stores to announce its arrival on the scene.

Adjusting supply and demand

While manufacturers have a vested interest in matching supply with demand, much of the work of doing so is handled at the retail level. As was discussed previously, retail architecture is routinely used to create spaces that help sellers assess the preferences of their customers. These might be listening corners in a music shop, dressing rooms in a clothing boutique or spaces where customers can order customized goods. However, these architectural features are not the only means by which shops can adjust supply and demand. They can also contribute directly to the redefinition of certain aspects of supply by influencing demand in a specific and dynamic way. Such retail spaces are designed to experiment with or test on a larger scale, that area which exists between a supply of goods and the demand for them. It is in this ephemeral area where new ideas are introduced and consumer desires are shaped.

Like the sneak preview of a film or the unveiling of a concept car, the shops that explore this terrain want to use what is on display to shape consumer demand for those products to come. For example, so-called Guerrilla stores like those set up by Comme des Garçons shape consumer preferences with their displays more than with what they actually sell. Whether visitors make a purchase or not, they will take their newfound preferences with them when they go to shop in more conventional boutiques at a later time. Guerilla stores experiment with the relationship between products and tastes, redefining the demand that will ultimately manifest itself in regular shops. In more precise terms, the connection that these shops seek to create with customers is more than just commercial in nature; it also encompasses conceptual art and ideas about fashion and lifestyle. The presence of something in this kind of market space is therefore never neutral in the sense that anything displayed there automatically serves to modify demand in some way. The avant-garde architecture in Prada's boutique does nothing if not emphasize the avant-garde nature of the products for sale there, all the while prescribing a correspondingly specific notion of taste and thereby influencing demand.

The shop makes the market

Ultimately, the three aspects of market function articulated to this point should be considered not as steps *per se*, but as guidelines for conceiving of and reading retail architecture. What is more, locations in and of themselves can never deploy all aspects of their potential market functions, and they should therefore not be thought of as the simple sum of commercial decisions made beforehand and elsewhere. They should, rather, be thought of in terms of what they contribute, as spaces, to the concrete production of the market relationship. Even if retail architecture constitutes but one aspect of this relationship, it constitutes much more than the simple manifestation of commercial strategies in space. The shop makes the market, which is to say that it partly produces the relationship between a clientele and a supply of goods. These two objects are joined by the way it presents products, attracts customers and generally organizes their convergence.

In acquiring customers, organizing their movements and trajectories and in encouraging their loyalty, shops suggest modes of choice, not just receiving customers, but actually shaping them. The specificity of the shop lies in its ability as a location (that is, a place apart from what is outside) and as a space (that is, a place that is organized spatially), to bring together three elements: products, customers and markets. The shop must give context to the products it offers for sale, such as by highlighting their homogeneity or heterogeneity. It must bring customers into proximity with the products so that they feel a connection with them, usually as a result of the products' style, its method of consumption or uses. Finally, by bringing together certain products and certain customers, the shop creates a market, one that is unique and confined to the shop itself.

Whatever else it may do, the essential task of the shop as a market space is to convert visitors into customers, even if the purchase is made at another time in another location. Along these lines, the first contribution of the commercial space is to incite the otherwise passive spectator, curious individual or 'scene seeker' to make choices that will lead to a transaction. This transformation can be aided by the configuration of objects and spaces within the store, the use of sound, perfume or lighting or access to boutique credit cards. In turning visitors into customers, one of the more complex aspects of the shop that arises is its status as a public space. It is, after all, a space that is open to the public, even if the degree of its openness can vary (as determined by the arrangement and decoration of storefronts, windows and doors). However, at the same time, the shop is not the kind of public space that can be visited like any other – a visit there may well be a means of something, but it must also be an end in itself – shopping can also be a leisure activity that involves visiting shops as an end in itself.

However, from a marketing point of view, the shop visit must be managed in such a way that those visiting know to attribute a particular identity to the owner of the establishment, namely that of merchant. Merchant identity has progressively changed over the course of retail history, and it did so particularly with the rise of chain stores, global retailers and business models like franchising. All of these businesses blur the line between merchant and manufacturer, a result of which is that customers today no longer find it necessary to know the identity of the individual owner as it was the case in old-fashioned boutiques where the retail relationship was based on loyalty.

The public/private nature of the shop can be reconciled by thinking of it as a space that is open to the public, but only conditionally so. Visitors enlist the shop to help them navigate a market relationship, one that is decidedly private. The art of shop design is to create a welcoming entrance or to blur the border between the public space of the street and the semi-public space of the shop. Some of the tactics used by architects to accomplish this is to extend the shop window into an entrance hall such as Grayson's, which draw shoppers into the store almost without them noticing (fig. 2.8). There are also strategies that involve opening boutiques directly onto public space, thereby making customers unsure of whether they are in the boutique or out. Customers standing outside the shop looking into its windows are already in the position of buyer: they are hesitating whether to buy or not. The more steps they take into the shops, the more removed they become from being the simple passer-by: they are debating whether to buy this or that product. That is why the design of the entryway devoted to this anticipated and hard-won transformation may be considered the cornerstone of retail architecture.

However, simply crossing the threshold is not enough, because the client must then be made to feel some kind of attachment, however ephemeral, to the attributes of the products on display. That is to say, inside the shop, the customer must find the basis of a quasi-private relationship with those products. All retail architecture may be interpreted as a market medium that allows retail places to suggest different ways of associating products and organize the meeting between buyers and sellers, but, throughout the very short time of the transaction, it also presents most of the different devices of market mediations. Some of them are directly attached to the supply side but will leave the shop arena to follow the customer outside the boutique (brands, labels, logo, products), others are directly attached to the customer and will enter with him into the boutique (social status,

2.8 Grayson: view from the
outside towards the sunken
shop window

budget, family preferences and so forth). It is probably the capacity
of the different architectural settings within the shop to perform
most of those different market devices that can explain part of the
retail architecture's efficiency to attract customers and produce
economic performance.

33 The shop as market space

03
The vicissitudes of the boutique
Introduction to the case studies
and interviews
David Vernet and Leontine de Wit

3.1 Frontage of Exinger
slaughterhouse, Vienna

1
L. Montigny, quoted in
N. Pevsner, 'Shops, Stores and
Department Stores', in *A History
of Building Types*, Princeton,
NJ: Princeton University Press,
1976, p. 263

The concept of the 'boutique' has taken a variety of forms, as is proved by the numerous meanings this French word has acquired over time, meanings that sometimes have been complete opposites. For a long time, this was the definition of a generic retail space, a storage place and the space adjacent where goods were sold. In the nineteenth century, however, the definition became more explicit, and came to depict an outlet reserved for the growing middle classes,[1] which sold luxury or tailored products (clothes, perfumes, delicacies) to suit an exclusive lifestyle. The term was used in this way world-wide until the 1950s when, as a reaction to the advent of large-scale retailing, it came to be used to denote a small outlet, generally for women, owned by an independent proprietor, who is still capable of offering treasures infrequently found anywhere else. Indeed, the word 'boutique' has been reserved for market sectors not involved in or threatened by mass production and consumption: the speciality shops.

At the same time, large international companies have begun to describe their outlets as 'boutiques' while they are, technically speaking, chain stores. By doing so, they have assigned certain qualities to the boutique and attempted to take advantage of the exclusivity the term has come to represent. This evolution in semantics says something about the evolution of retail itself. All in all, with the shift in concept from a generic shop to one that is upmarket and class-oriented, and subsequently to a marketing tool, the boutique has become a handy hold-all concept. Its main characteristics seem to offer the promise of a relationship not based solely on commerce, but also on additional benefits such as advice, exclusivity and service. For business, this definition is attractive, and covers a range of diverse, contemporary retail environments. The case studies presented here aim to investigate the elements that are common to these various concepts and that can explain the continuing success of the boutique.

2
*Le trésor de la langue française
informatisé*, Online. Available
http://atilf.atilf.fr/dendien/
scripts/tlfiv5/visusel.exe?44;s=
50176095;r=1;nat=;sol=1;
(accessed 30 March 2006)

The word *boutique* appeared for the first time in French in 1242.[2] It derived from the Ancient Provençal term *botiga*, which originated from the Greek word for storage: *apotheke* (literally: 'a place where things are put away', from *apo-* 'away' and *tithenai* 'to put'). In contrast to its synonym, *magasin*, which is still used in French to define either a storage place or a shop, the term 'boutique' quickly evolved to denote only the selling space. In addition, unlike *magasin*, it has taken on a secondary symbolic connotation, and refers not only to the built environment where commerce takes place, but also to the social activity that originates from and gravitates around this place. 'Boutique' is used to describe social interactions linked to the act of buying and selling, and a lot of familiar business-related expressions have incorporated the term.[3] The importance of the symbolic meaning of the word probably accounts for the pejorative connotation boutique has had for a long time, because of the supposedly narrow-minded and secretive behaviour of shopkeepers (*un esprit boutiquier*).

3
'Tenir boutique', to practise a
trade; 'plier boutique', to cease any
activity;' parler boutique', to speak
about professional matters

35 The vicissitudes of the boutique

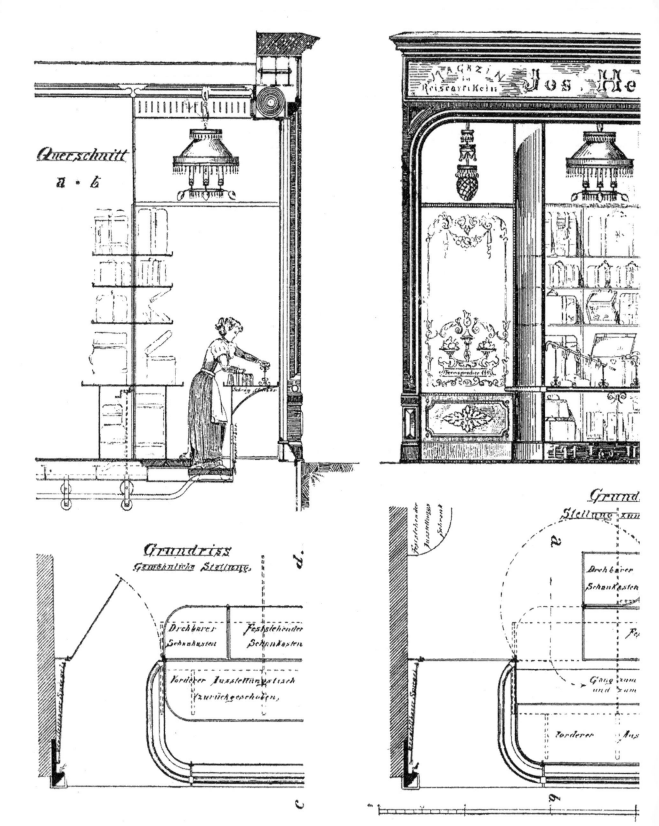

3.2 Jos. Hermanns boutique in Cologne:
section through the shop window (around 1886)

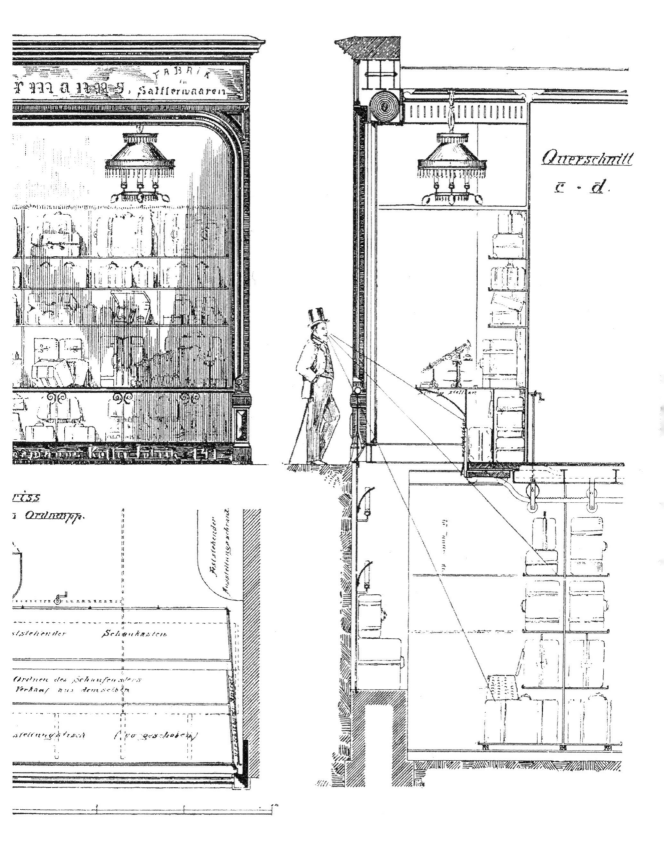

FABRIK für Sattlerwaaren

Querschnitt c - d

4
Pevsner, op. cit., p. 251–72

The architectural development of shops happened at a slow pace. In his book *A History of Building Types*, published in 1976, Nicolaus Pevsner analysed the transformation of architectural styles in response to social and cultural changes, and their evolution and different approaches to function, materials or style. Pevsner specifically focuses on the nineteenth century, a crucial period for diversification of architecture styles. In the chapter entitled 'Shops, stores and department stores',[4] he analyses larger stores, such as arcades or department stores; their emergence had a major effect on both city patterns and different forms of retail. He also argues that the boutique and small-scale shops followed a slow development to the end of the nineteenth century (fig. 3.1). Nevertheless, this evolution is worth studying, as it is the basis for and explains the main transformations in nineteenth-century retailing.

There has been some consistency in the way retail architecture has evolved from two types the market stall and the shop. Historically, the markets have marked the pattern of most cities, in the form of squares, but the construction of market stalls has always remained more or less unchanged. The shop, on the other hand, was not visible in the urban footprint, but the improvement of this typology has gone through a series of technological and organizational changes.

Until the late eighteenth century, technological advances aimed at achieving two goals: a more effective use of available surfaces (including maximizing their use) and improved 'communication' between the spaces (public domain) and the customer. The use of glass has been a major factor in this development. Used in architecture since Roman times, glass was not used consistently in retail until the 1200s, when the technique of crown or leaded glass was developed. This technique, where a glass ball was blown and then flattened, produced small panes that were joined with lead strips and pieced together to create windows. Glass remained a great luxury, however. Since glass at this stage was translucent rather than transparent, allowing some light to enter the shop premises, it proved insufficient to change the way goods were displayed. In the late seventeenth century, the invention of plate glass made it possible to produce large surfaces (a new process developed in France in 1688, originally for the mirror industry[5]). Glazed shop fronts appeared, first in Holland, and eventually became common in Europe around the 1850s.[6] Transparent shop windows had a profound effect on retail, as they allowed better lighting of spaces further away from the façade; it then became possible to use deeper spaces, and to draw clients further into the shop. This development gained force in the late nineteenth century through the introduction of gas and electric lighting (fig. 3.2). In addition, the use of glass fundamentally transformed the construction and layout of shops, allowing larger openings onto the street and therefore a better display of goods.

The evolution of other construction materials allowed building elements to become lighter and stronger, and to perform better.

5
A Brief History of Glass, Online. Available www.glass online.com/ infoserv/history.html (accessed 30 March 2006)

6
K.A. Morrison, *English Shops and Shopping: An Architectural History*, New Haven, CT: Yale University Press, 2003, p. 41–66

7
Ibid., p. 28

8
Coined by designer James Pilditch, in 1961, primarily to define the role of packaging. See J. Pilditch, *The Silent Salesman: How to Develop Packaging That Sells*, London: Business Books Ltd, 1973

9
G. Richardson, *Medieval Guild*, Online. Available http://eh. net/encyclopedia/article/ richardson.guilds (accessed 13 February 2006)

10
Streets still bear the marks of these spaces with names such as 'the Butchers' Street'

11
There were earlier proto-examples such as the Exeter Exchange in London, built in 1566

Starting in the late 1770s and reaching a climax in 1851, with Paxton's Crystal Palace, the introduction of cast iron structures and roofs is a good example of how technology can transform an economic activity. In fact, by diminishing the width of and increasing the distance between load-bearing walls, a larger surface was available for the retail floors of shops. This tendency was reinforced by the continuous transformation of land ownership: adjacent lots were joined together to form larger shops,[7] and this maximization of space allowed the use of the first floor as a sale surface.

In addition to these material and structural innovations, more sophisticated techniques for display were introduced. The generic expression 'silent salesmen'[8] is used to describe a number of practices, ranging from marketing tools (advertisements, merchandising) to product-based innovations (packaging, price tags), to retail equipment or furniture. The common purpose of these was to reduce the work of and need for shop staff. Architecturally, changes to spaces such as the reception area, counters, a cash desk or shop signs went a long way to increasing the autonomy of the customer, and have become aspects specific to the boutique.

Two social, political and technological movements, however, deeply influenced most aspects of European societies by the end of the eighteenth century. They also changed the way businesses were managed and given form. These new changes were quite different from the kind of technological transformations that small shops faced.

The first event, ushered in by the French Revolution and the subsequent introduction of free trade legislation, was the liberation of shopkeepers from the influence of the rigid guild system.[9] Guilds had, up to that point, ensured a spatial homogeneity: businesses of the same kind were concentrated in the same district.[10] With the disappearance of these restrictions, it became possible for shops to move and to look for new forms of cooperation, but now in any location within their cities.

Arcades can be seen as the innovative urban form induced by this liberalization. Since shops were no longer grouped by function, as they had been in the pre-modern city, they could be located according to the social structure they were serving. The first comprehensive example was the *Galerie de Bois*, a temporary wooden structure erected in 1786 beside the Palais-Royal in Paris.[11] This arcade proved so successful that it was rebuilt, with permanent materials, in 1829.

Arcades were extremely suitable for retail. Indeed, they provided independent shop owners with an ideal location: under one roof, one could find a variety of products, different yet complementary, such as clothing and hosiery, millinery and confectionery. The public spaces, now sheltered under glazed roofs, became new pedestrian lanes through the city, and provided an optimal location for shop fronts. Potential customers remained for longer periods in these spaces;

3.3 Schein carpet store in
Vienna (architects, Fellner &
Helmer, 1896)

12
As an example: L.-F. Céline,
Journey to the End of the Night,
trans. R. Mannheim, New York:
New Directions, 1983, p. 65–6

13
J.L. Wingert, *La vie après le pétrole*,
Paris: éditions Autrement, 2005,
p. 130–2

14
For a broader analysis of both
types, refer to the Annotated
Bibliography on pp. 150–159

15
R.D. Tamilia, *The Wonderful World
of the Department Store in
Historical Perspective*, Online,
2002. Available http://faculty.
quinnipiac.edu/charm/dept.store.
pdf (accessed 27 December 2005)

new functions (for instance, cafés or tea salons) became linked to retail. Each function helped to strengthen the other, competition gave way to cooperation, a sort of virtuous circle. In fact, the development of arcades was not the invention of a new kind of shop; instead it was the reshuffling of existing forms. Literature demonstrates this when descriptions of the life in the arcades are likened to scenes from street life.[12]

The second event to extensively transform retail, in general, and the boutique in particular, was the Industrial Revolution. The Industrial Revolution first emerged in England in the second half of the eighteenth century, and progressively spread throughout Europe. It brought about changes in both the production and distribution of goods. Factors such as the increased speed of manufacturing (due to better use of energy[13]), the extension of the railway system and the use of steam machines to produce machine tools all led to a fundamental shift in how retailing was organized. These changes had several consequences. The first was the clear separation between functions: between public areas and the shopkeeper's household, and between the production and selling areas. As a result, outlets stopped being 'shops' (where goods are sold adjacent to the workshops where they are produced) and became 'stores' (the sales area is a place to store goods produced somewhere else). The second was the emergence of new types of retailing, each time focused on being more competitive, with different spatial and distributive characteristics. Examples include department stores or commercial malls.[14] These new forms of retail permitted the development and use of new advances (the role of 'silent salesmen' became more important in these new environments, eventually leading to self-service in the 1930s); above all, they introduced a radical change in scale (fig. 3.3). These developments did not necessarily clash with the boutique: there are numerous examples of independent shopkeepers who were able to adapt. For instance, department stores leased space to individual merchants, and the boutique model played a role in the development of commercial malls.[15] In fact, boutiques adapted and took other forms in these large locations. In department stores, they became stalls, shops-in-a-shop or private salons. In commercial malls, which in many respects can be described as suburban arcades, boutiques took advantage of links to the outside, and of innovative stock and supply management. As boutiques worked to define their role in new environments, department stores and commercial malls permitted them to evolve and demonstrate that it was possible to mix different types and scales.

In the twentieth century, the boutique still appears in different forms: it still emerges as an independent speciality shop, avoiding pressures of scaling-up, of urban concentration and changes in location. Also, it may have adapted to these new conditions, by becoming one component of a department store or commercial mall.

16
M.H. Seid, *Where It All Began: The Evolution of Franchising,* Online. Available www.msaworldwide. com/upload/History%20of%20 Franchising.pdf> (accessed 4 January 2006)

The phenomenon that changed the very nature of the boutique is the introduction in the post-war United States of the chain store model. The return of millions of soldiers and the subsequent baby boom created a demand for all types of products and services. Chain stores, often in the form of franchised outlets, turned out to be the ideal business model for the rapid expansion of retailing, first for the hotel/motel and food industries, then for convenience goods and services.[16] Franchising and chain stores had existed long before the 1940s, but when the American economy secured its position as an international leader in the 1950s and 1960s, these models expanded drastically.

Chain stores did impact spatially on small-scale shops. For instance, as centralized marketing and purchasing eliminated the need for extensive storage, the entire ground floor surface was made available for retailing. But most of all, chain stores introduced a new role for the boutique. Boutiques were no longer necessarily bound to one owner, as they could be owned by a company or a franchise. The traditional link with the shopkeeper disappeared while, at the same time, it was still consciously exploited in advertisements. Merchants cleverly made use of some of the traditional characteristics of the boutique, (such as uniqueness, exclusiveness, warmth and attentive service), so as to increase the attractiveness of chain stores. The emphasis shifted to the image of the boutique: this allowed global economic and management systems to hide behind a mask of authenticity and uniqueness. The boutique had become a concept.

Diverse forms of the boutique co-exist in modern retail and though they represent concurrent, and sometimes opposite business models, they still share a common name. When analysing what is called a 'boutique', it might be of benefit to have a look at this diversity, and through the diversity to explain what retailing is, how it functions and what tools are available to achieve commercial success. This desire to look at a cross-section of contemporary retail architecture led to the selection of the case studies presented here. Some of the shops analysed might not fit completely into the category of a 'boutique', but they nevertheless cast light on some key elements of retail: the Grayson shop, for instance, illustrates the main characteristics of a 1940s chain store; in the showroom Flos, one comes across constant re-branding, the same architect providing a face lift to the same premises over a period of 40 years.

Another criterion used to choose the cases was their relevance over a period of time. The cases selected cover a period of over 110 years, and this time span is sufficient to make note of differences or similarities in the way shops have evolved in the face of cultural, historical, social and economic changes.

In order to break down retailing into logical sections, seven features of stores have been chosen: SOCIAL ISSUES, SALES, LOCATION, DESIGNER/CLIENT, MATERIALS, DISPLAY and COMMUNICATION.

They represent the major mechanisms at play in a boutique. The aim of identifying common features is to aid in the comparison between cases that are distinctly different, but manage to come up with different solutions to the same problem (how to deal with a display, for instance). Only the most salient features of each case have been analysed, and the analysis is therefore incomplete. When difficulties arose in clearly distinguishing an aspect of a shop, as it fell under two criteria, the most relevant feature was selected.

Of the seven criteria applied, SOCIAL ISSUES and SALES are features that relate to the porosity of the boutique to historical, cultural and economic changes. Still, the oldest example selected here (the Pfund dairy shop, built in 1891) and one of the most recent (the 2002 Australian Homemade Ice Cream outlet) share strong similarities, in both the floor layout, as well as display techniques. Contextual, historical criteria are not sufficient to determine the range of tools shopkeepers have at their disposal. The five other features relate to the enduring nature of the boutique, separate from the business models involved. The seven features can be described as follows.

SOCIAL ISSUES

While some architects define retailing as the ultimate form of socialization (and, some would argue, the only one left), it is, without doubt, one of the oldest. Shops have always been sensitive and responsive to transformations in society, either reflecting them, or offering an environment in which they can be expressed. This responsiveness, depending on the case, can be called a commercial strategy, a rebellion, a political statement or any combination of these.

SALES

New sales techniques are essential in most shops, as commercial success is always paramount. Some outlets are particularly good at implementing new, innovative approaches that can take material, spatial or behavioural form. Stores try to distance themselves from old, out-of-date approaches, and new sales techniques are the result of attempts to achieve constant improvements. 'Sales' refers to the differences and similarities between various business systems (shop-in-shop, specialty shop, chain stores).

LOCATION

A location allows a shopkeeper to fine-tune the shop to its target group. Location influences the types of products sold, but also the types of accessibility required. While most of the shops tend to try to be located in prominent places, there are several examples to the contrary that demonstrate that the benefits of visibility are not always straightforward. The relation between public and private spheres, a notion linked to cultural contexts, is also studied under this theme.

DESIGNER/CLIENT

The link between the boutique and its owner is fundamental in most of the examples selected. Also, clients are an essential driving force: they have a specific image of what the shop should be and select shops based on a mixture of financial, commercial and aesthetic criteria.

Shop designers not only can be architects; some are artists and industrial designers (especially since the 1980s). Entrepreneurs, and even clients, can be behind a shop design. In some cases, the designer will introduce new designs that permanently influence retailing.

MATERIALS

Materials and lighting are rarely neutral; they very often reflect social movements. Retailing has occasionally led to the development of new designs. Lighting is remarkable in this regard: its role has been extremely important in shops where it is used to expose (or hide) goods in an aesthetically desirable manner. Advances in lighting have occurred as a result of experimentation by retailers.

DISPLAY

Display techniques are of major importance in retailing, as they are the primary tools a shopkeeper can use to exhibit products or services. Here as well, technological advances have introduced innovations in the way goods are presented. A display is rarely neutral; its design is always related to the nature of the good (its size and shape) and its supposed value (availability, stylishness, ease of use). Displays often allow retailers to create environments that suggest certain behaviours.

COMMUNICATION

This generic term covers all the tools used by retailers to connect spatially to the external environment and to advertise products or services. Communication is always of major importance, and includes elements such as the entrance to the store, the façade the shop window, but also signs and advertising. Economic development and new forms of media have increased the exposure of retailing. The increase of advertising space in newspapers and on street furniture; the advent of the Internet and e-shopping, have all forced most retailers to rethink their sphere of influence. Boutiques are a single link in the chain of shops.

Nevertheless, no matter how good a design might be, a shop can never be reduced to only its physical appearance or location. Any retail design is conceived within economic limitations, and these are of major importance. The two interviews presented play a dual role: they describe the set-up of a boutique and the conditions that influence the boutique's coming of age. Also, and probably more importantly, the interviews highlight the economic dimensions of retail design, those intangible factors that drive architecture to try to reconcile certain tensions and contradictions.

Ultimately, both the case studies and interviews demonstrate that retailing is more than just architecture. A boutique is the result of a fine balance between social, material and economic factors, each time in different proportions and still of equal relevance. Curiously enough, in commerce, *trial and error* seems to be the rule, and intuition plays an important role. But the form that a boutique takes is nothing more than a response to one of the oldest human activities, and the uncertainty related to it.

04
Merchandising for gatherers
Interview with Oep Schilling and
Vincent Sturkenboom, G-Star
David Vernet

4.1 G-Star store in Liège,
Belgium

G-Star is a denim brand based in Amsterdam, the Netherlands. Its recent growth and international expansion have changed the rules of the game: among other things, a re-evaluation of the retail network proved necessary. Oep Schilling and Vincent Sturkenboom, who are both part of the Interiors Department, take a look at their work, the transformation of the retail side of the business in recent years, expectations for future development and the company's plans for keeping pace with it.

Please tell us something about G-Star and explain the type of distribution system you are currently using.

> *Oep Schilling*: We started G-Star in 1989. We currently employ 500 people: 250 at our headquarters in Amsterdam and the rest in sales offices and showrooms located in nineteen countries.

Until recently, there had been no need for mono-brand shops in Northern Europe, because of a dense network of multi-brand retail points. G-Star has taken advantage of these points from the beginning and still does today. They comprise around 4,500 of our clients. However, some countries seem to be less suitable for selling in multi-brand environments, or have less developed networks of multi-brand shops. In light of this situation, six years ago we developed a concept for G-Star mono-brand outlets. After finalizing the concept and finding a franchise partner, we opened the first G-Star Raw Store in Lyons five years ago.

What's the normal procedure for opening a mono-brand shop?

Oep Schilling: We have a team of around twenty dedicated people who are responsible for opening our mono-brand shops. By the end of 2005, we had opened thirty-eight outlets world-wide, in cities large and small – anywhere we found a promising market for G-Star. Each time we open a mono-brand shop, we look for a local partner, because they are more likely to have extensive knowledge of the market in question, which makes them better able to assess the risks involved (fig. 4.1).

In theory, it could be possible to open a shop in three months. However, because we work with partners who are asked to make a considerable investment, and who are responsible for on-site work and for communication with local authorities, we prefer to take the time to allow them to deal with this in the best possible way. It takes preparation and training and most of the time all this is new to the partner. We prefer to be thorough and to do it right rather than to rush things.

The ideal time frame from the moment we know the location until the actual opening is six months. Roughly, one or two months to design and draft the project, a month to negotiate and discuss with the local partner and three months working with local architects and contractors. This includes the time we spend on considering tenders and so forth. I'd say that the actual building of the shop accounts for ten–twelve weeks. During the fortnight leading up to the opening, the shop is furnished and, finally, stocked with merchandise.

Although you're working with franchised partners, all design aspects are the responsibility of G-Star. Can you elaborate?

Oep Schilling: The other day I showed some clients around our headquarters, and it made me realize that we do everything in-house. Our design process is very participative: people from different departments share their ideas about shop architecture with us.

We think that someone entering our shop should have an instant overview, should understand what he sees and should have no trouble setting off in the right direction. It's an elementary yet essential aspect of the interior design.

Vincent Sturkenboom: We communicate the G-Star concept in a similar way world-wide. The only differences from country to country are due to specific regulations and requirements – building regulations, opening times and such – and this factor has an influence on certain aspects of the shop. We try not to copy ourselves, and there's always room for a side step. But it should be clear that you're in a G-Star Store, whether in Barcelona or in LA.

And how do you go about renewing the concept?

Vincent Sturkenboom: It's all about evolution. The concept we're developing now is the first one for the G-Star Raw brand. It's evolving, but I'd say that rather than trying to transform it, our aim is to promote its development as a brand-new concept in the next five years.

Oep Schilling: First, we try things. Although G-Star Stores should be essentially the same all over the world, we still want the first shop to be somewhat different from the last one. Strategically, the smart thing to do is to make each outlet look slightly different, while still bearing the traces of a constant evolution. That way, you won't need to refurbish all of them at once – at a point when they're suddenly all outdated.

How would you describe the purpose of a shop? It's obviously there to sell your products, but some companies use the shop to convey brand image. What's your position on this matter?

Vincent Sturkenboom: I see it as a play. Our stores should be like a stage, a backdrop for what happens. It's part of the play, but the actors – in the form of our products – are more important. You need a space in which to sell your wares and that space should be accessible to a wide range of potential customers.

Oep Schilling: I think the main thing is to create the right environment for our merchandise and for the customer. Of course it's important to convey our image at the same time, but it should not disturb the selling process. We're always looking for consensus without a loss of quality. We want the public to see us as a high-end jeans manufacturer (fig. 4.2), but we also want to keep our customers as they grow older – in other words, to operate in the mainstream market. We think that the person who wears jeans at 30 will still be wearing jeans at 55.

What role does architectural design play in your shops?

Oep Schilling: We aim for long-term consistency, which means that whether a customer enters one of our older shops – let's say in Paris – or a new one, perhaps in Sidney, the experience is the same. Maybe it's on an unconscious level, but it feels like G-Star. We were amazed by the success of our first shops. In countries where we're known, it's

4.2 Handcrafted objects are
used in fashion shows and for
window dressing in stores
world-wide, testifying to
G-Star tailoring abilities

4.3 The denim wall in Liège,
Belgium

4.4 G-Star store in New York

4.5 Interior of G-Star store
in New York

4.6 Detail of a display
element

4.7 Façade of G-Star store in
Edinburgh

been easier. In global hubs like New York (fig. 4.4), Paris, Barcelona and other spots targeted by cheap tourist flights, our shops perform perfectly. It's harder in smaller cities, but sales figures show that our average sales per square metre have been better than expected.

This simply means that when customers recognize us and find us, everything else falls into place. The merchandise has to be good, because, in the end, that's what sells. The architectural design contributes to create the right setting. Our only spatial distinction is that between menswear and womenswear. Even though we feature several programmes in one collection, they are not relegated to specific areas. We focus on each line by means of visual merchandising. If you make a very beautiful shop with too little room for merchandising, what's it worth? The reverse is true as well. If you make a space that revolves entirely around merchandising, you don't achieve the image you want to convey. The emotional part (it should feel and look good), the practical part (it should work and be functional) and the financial part are all important and decisive.

Architecturally, we try to be consistent. Ultimately, however, the sales department is leading; if, at a certain point, they think that something different will lead to an increase in sales, we will to follow their suggestion. Of course, this will provoke a discussion, and we will participate in that discussion defending the design aspect. But if they say, 'Now, we need something yellow', yellow it will be! It's an ongoing battle between pragmatism and design.

How do you implement the balance between merchandising and architecture in the shop?

Vincent Sturkenboom: Orientation is an important part of entering the shop. Each shop has three essential components: a *denim wall* (fig. 4.3), a cash desk and fitting rooms. At the moment, we consider the *denim wall* the most important. The idea behind it is quite simple: the shopper should think, 'If I can't find jeans here, I can't find them anywhere.'

As studies have shown that circulation in retail spaces is similar from store to store, we keep this information in mind when creating an interior. We try to develop our spatial concept the same way in each location. A vital factor is existing architecture, which we want to leave intact, while also blending our concept into what is already there. Part of our approach is to think in big areas. We make large walls, large volumes and large boxy elements, avoiding the repetition of materials – reserving concrete for the floor, for instance – to achieve a balance between materials and volumes (fig. 4.5). Our range of materials is limited and simple: raw oak, concrete, black and untreated steel and black MDF with or without lacquer. We apply only a few colours to the walls.

Oep Schilling: Since a brand expresses itself through visual merchandising, including displays, we constantly study how to incorporate this kind of communication into our shops, by means of a one-to-one relationship between product and architecture (fig. 4.6).

Could you explain the use of displays, furniture and lighting in your shops?

Oep Schilling: About 95 per cent of the furniture and display units in our shops comes from existing stock. When we need something specific or new for a location, we make it. If we think it's good and reusable, we add it to our in-house catalogue, upgrading it from 'special' to 'standard'. All interior furnishings are produced in the Netherlands, stored at the factory and shipped to given locations as needed. We'll continue to introduce new materials annually, but not all at once.

Vincent Sturkenboom: Light is part of the concept and has many functions to fulfil. It has to reflect the correct colour and appearance of products, while also appealing to the customer. People have to feel good, to be attracted while still outside and to be tempted to enter the shop. It's important to us to have the entire shop function as a display window. Passers-by strolling along should be able to see the denim wall and the complete interior, front to back. To achieve this objective, we opt for a façade that's as open as possible and for an interior that's illuminated well enough to be visible, open and inviting (fig. 4.7).

G-Star gained in popularity after exhibiting at trade fairs. Is there a relationship between retail architecture and the design of trade fair stands?

Oep Schilling: Although the same team of designers is involved in both stands and shops, each type of project demands a different approach. The trade fair is all about image. You have to make a statement. Shop design combines three factors: image, merchandising and customer. We look at showrooms and trade fairs as laboratories that help us to define the desired G-Star environment. Both give us an opportunity to get feedback and to react to client response.

Vincent Sturkenboom: Fairs allow us to refine the direction we'll be taking in coming years, to see what works and what doesn't. Retail outlets, on the other hand, have a completely different function. There, it's about more than image. What we learn at the fairs goes into our shops.

Oep Schilling: At a fair, you are often located next to one or more competitors. When you're operating in the same market, identity is important. Our clients are looking for brand identity. Developing a brand image for fairs has helped make G-Star Stores as recognizable as possible (fig. 4.8).

4.8 G-Star showroom

How are you preparing for the future?

> *Oep Schilling*: We're investigating new developments in technology, of
> course, such as radio frequency identification (RFI) and the possibility
> for customers to visit the shop, pay for their purchases and have their
> orders shipped to any destination. That's the technical side of our job.
> We know that such technologies are already being used for things as
> diverse as stock management in the retail business to the nightlife
> industry. But I think many people still see shopping as a kind of
> entertainment, and entertainment demands an environment. The need
> for amusement is instinctive. It goes really deep and the shop interior
> is the perfect place to cater to that need.

5.1 Champs Elysées, Paris:
interior

Louis Vuitton is the main brand of LVMH, the world-leading
consortium in luxury goods. The recent opening of its flagship store in
Paris has been fiercely debated, owing in part to its exuberance and to
the use of art in a commercial environment (fig. 5.1). Meanwhile, the
company's in-house architects continue to build shops and boutiques at
high speed. Based in Paris and directed by Eric Carlson and David
McNulty, the LV Architecture Department manages large numbers of
projects in forty-nine countries. The size and financial power of the
company, along with its dense network of boutiques, make for very
special working conditions. Recently, Eric Carlson discussed the details
of his work.

**The LV Architecture Department has undergone many changes recently.
Can you explain why?**

Having worked at LV for five years, David McNulty and
I are currently taking a more overt approach to architectural issues.
Previously, the work consisted of managing the externally realized
interior designs of stores ranging from 60 to 100 m². The strategy
was to develop an image and repeat it everywhere. Back then,
everybody thought it was the best way to communicate brand
identity: from petrol stations to McDonald's to fashion labels and
so on. Even though there was less global travel, it was comforting
for people to find brands portrayed in the same way everywhere
they went. But things have changed. We're more sophisticated.
We travel more. We come into contact with more things more often,
through magazines or various forms of communication. And so we
want more.

There's another reason, a very practical one. When LV introduced
ready-to-wear fashion and shoes into the product line, in addition to its
traditional leather goods, store sizes tripled. As the product line grew,
we had to find bigger spaces, and suddenly we were forced to deal with
architectural factors such as the structural, spatial and exterior aspects
of retail design. The façade – something of an architectural by-product

5.2 Nagoya (architect,
J. Aoki)

of the commercial strategy – became the first element of experimentation. And because of building, cultural and historical constraints, as well as budget issues in different zones and different profit margins, the same façade cannot be repeated everywhere. Independently, and at a separate pace, the increase in surface area affected our store interiors as well. The previously homogenous, one-floor volumes were no longer valid, and new architectural elements, such as stairs, became important.

Beginning in 1998, we designed the Osaka project and Jun Aoki designed the Nagoya project (fig. 5.2), both of which were very well received. I think those in charge realized that architecture has an enormous impact on the perception of a store, as well as on the functional aspect. And instead of us having to push them, they began

57 Interview: Eric Carlson, Louis Vuitton

to push us. All of a sudden what used to be an interior cookie-cutter concept encountered the need for variety, in terms of architecture, and became an opportunity to express brand identity.

How is your department handling the new situation?

The in-house team has a staff of twenty-three, seventeen of whom are architects, 30 per cent non-French. The office is divided into four geographical zones: Asia/Pacific, Japan, the Americas (including South Africa) and Europe (including the Middle East). Each has three to five architects and a logistics person. There is also a group of four people dedicated to the development of furniture and to liaisons with manufacturers. In charge of construction quality and schedules are construction-management teams at our LV offices in Paris (fig. 5.3), Hong Kong and New York; and, independently, Higo & Associates in Tokyo.

A continuum of activity within the international network of 314 directly controlled stores includes new construction, renovation and expansion, resulting in the annual design and realization of a total of 50 to 100 projects. This means that one or two stores open each week, ranging in size from 100 to 1000 m^2 and in complexity from interior fit-out to free-standing building.

5.4 1:1 prototype of a façade

5.5 Roppongi (architects,
A. Clementi, J. Aoki, LV
Architecture Department)

A unique aspect of the work is our dual role as both client and architect. Around 20 per cent of the store projects are designed internally. These generally include projects that provide an opportunity for the architectural exploration of façades, structures or atypical spatial conditions. This type of project is more common in Japan or Asia, simply because luxury-retail neighbourhoods in European and American cities are often limited by constraints related to historical conservation.

For the remaining 80 per cent of projects, we work with external architects, and our task is to act as translators between the architects and the senior executives involved. This dual role is highly unusual and allows us to go faster than everybody else: after coming up with an idea and making a decision, we can move forward immediately. It's a distinctive process and one in which we modify the typical developmental phase of retail design. Our approach to architecture reduces abstraction and the margin of error by enabling us to build full-scale mock-ups (fig. 5.4). And all because LV has the means and the money to do so. It's a different type of process, and it entails great reliance on contractors, big budgets and research into materials. In luxury retail, it sometimes makes more economic sense to pay extra – for air transport rather than other means of shipment, for 24-hour work shifts, for additional on-site labour and so forth – in order to complete the project at an earlier date. Often the profits outweigh the extra costs incurred by an accelerated schedule.

What makes luxury retail unique, and what is LV's brand strategy?

People who think the fashion world is based on a far-reaching strategy are wrong. In this particular business, I think you have to be very responsive to 'now'. The notions of fashion, merchandising and architecture have little in common. Fashion changes with the season, merchandising every three months and, in the luxury retail sector, architecture every six years on average. Obviously, each of the three moves to a different beat. Because our market is primarily about fashion, LV needs to understand a given situation quickly and to act on it immediately. The same applies to our stores.

In addition, luxury retail stores have to reconcile the conflicting commercial demands of exclusivity versus inclusiveness. Commercially, there's a desire to create an exclusive environment to which only a select few have access. But there's also a wish to attract more and more customers for the sake of financial growth. Fundamentally, this company survives by being savvy and smart, and by evolving and changing, in an attempt to stay ahead of competitors who are also savvy and smart. Rather than being a conscious choice, it's an evolutionary process tied to the circumstances of the situation. Everything evolves gradually, in a series of small steps. Our Roppongi shop (fig. 5.5) has taken us one step further, as it involves not only an interior and a façade, but also the furniture. Setting aside any preconception of architecture as a permanent construct, we tried to follow the rhythms of fashion and to create something flexible without losing the desired sense of quality. It's a laboratory project. We have to wait for the results before deciding how to take the following step or opting for a return to the previous style. We'll see how it functions, how the image evolves and how we feel about the relevance of designing a different store for each project. We're in the midst of an era of collaboration: Prada working with OMA and with Herzog and de Meuron, Hermès with Renzo Piano and Dior with Kazuyo Sejima. LV has worked with Aoki and Kuma, as well as with our in-house architects, but even though the designers differ, the design language

5.6 Omotesando

remains the same. It bears repeating: we want stores that are architecturally sophisticated and that boldly respond to the basic economic nature of a specific commercial sector: luxury retail.

You mentioned an in-house division spread over four geographical zones. Does each zone have different criteria, in terms of markets and target groups?

We do see the need for a culture- or site-specific approach to the market. In America, for instance, the whole notion of a VIP room is somewhat politically incorrect, but we still feel a need to cater to customers with more money to spend. There's definitely a paradox between needs related to culture and to commerce. Our store in Hawaii features a wooden partition between the retail space and the VIP room; made from chocolate-like components, the wall creates only a subtle distinction between the two areas and does nothing to disturb the overall sense of equality. (A more playful element at the store is a large lantern, afloat in midair, displaying a Hawaiian-shirt motif with leaves that form the LV monogram: a combination of Vuitton and Hawaii.)

Thus, we can say that a culture-specific approach sometimes corresponds to site-specific economic conditions. In Japan, customers don't want to pay for purchases in a conspicuously public area, as money is considered a private matter, so the cash desk appears at the rear of the shop. Chinese people don't like the idea of a credit card being carried to another part of the shop – who knows what might happen to it? – so all transactions are done in cash.

Are you involved with LV's other departments or with the artistic director?

In terms of the creative initiative, it's really our responsibility. We present our designs to the Store Committee, a body that is composed of the CEO and CFO of LV, the director of the Store Department and, whenever possible, the director of LV in the country where the project is to be built. They either approve the design or make comments and suggestions. Integrating the very specific concerns of these business people into our plans is critical to the programming of the project. Our talks revolve around their thoughts on the relevance of a design, on the likelihood of it increasing their annual sales, and on ways to stock the store efficiently and to facilitate restocking. All these things count. Fortunately, the committee members are deeply involved, very sensitive, highly creative people. Even so, it's our job to focus on conceptual factors, on the formal and spatial aspects of the store, on materials, on the location in terms of urban design, on the relationship between the store and its cultural context and, not least, on the impact of the store as a spatial experience. Architects tend to talk about the phenomenon of educating the client, but, by and large, it doesn't exist. Under normal circumstances, you can get a client to accept a certain degree of sophistication, and that's where it stops. If you spend time with him daily, however, or several days a week for years preceding the realization of a retail project, as we often do, it's possible to make the point that architecture plays an important role in the shopping experience.

As for merchandising, we have nothing to do with it. Merchandising aids, such as plans for window displays, are the responsibility of those in charge of the shop. We do discuss the look of the interior, though, during meetings held to develop new shop systems. One vital aspect of these talks is the hard line that's drawn between fixed elements and those that are mobile or changeable.

Do you achieve architectural continuity and uniformity in your shop designs?

For practical reasons usually linked to building regulations, the façade often needs to be designed before the retail space. Exterior and interior are separate projects. More limitations are imposed on the interior, because a certain level of repetition is needed to create a consistent environment and a space that reflects the history of the company.

One reason for choosing a layered façade emerged from the idea of doing something different from what our competitors have done. Everybody is doing glass or stone façades, and we wanted to introduce the notion of texture, which is what LV products are all about. But an even earlier and basically conceptual reason is that a double façade has allowed us to create mystery, a dreamlike atmosphere based on visual distortion. It's a very perceptual thing. The façade is tangible but not concrete. It's hard to speculate on its depth or materiality.

In 1998, we organized a competition for the Nagoya project and hired an external architect, Jun Aoki. He introduced a double layer of printed glass featuring the classic Louis Vuitton *damier* pattern. The resulting *moiré* effect adorns a virtually liquid façade that includes window displays, entrance, signage and service access. Because of its geometric simplicity, the *damier* motif became the inspiration for a series of skins on the façades of subsequent projects. The Nagoya project lent a new direction to LV architecture. We encourage architects to look at what's been done and to take it to the next level without hesitation. The Nagoya *moiré* glass façade, for example, inspired our design of the woven-metal and mosaic-tile façade for Seoul, which in turn inspired Aoki's design of the woven-metal-mesh and polished-metal façade in Omotesando (fig. 5.6).

What's so fascinating about the *moiré* phenomenon is that it combines otherwise ordinary materials into something special. And, indeed, effects created by an interesting skin and a mix of materials have become the medium that connects a series of buildings designed by different architects.

And this within the wide range of projects you deal with . . .

In the world of retail – of luxury retail – there are many criteria, very specific demands and an incredibly dense filter of constraints. You are right in implying that each store is different. Our shops make more money in certain areas and thus need a bigger back of the house, whereas in other areas, where property values are sky-high, you don't want to spend months of rent on the non-retail areas of a store when you can rely on one delivery every two days, two deliveries every two days or, as in Hong Kong, one delivery every four hours. It's not easy to produce good architecture with all these constraints. It's extremely hard, and for years and years heavy constraints precluded a real connection between design, architects and commercial retail architecture. Today, business people see the advantage of such a connection, and architects have found ways to manage all these variables. You see it happening. Retail design is a new, functional typology that's gradually attracting more and more architects. It's exciting.

I also want to stress, however, the practical side of a luxury retailer's commercial dealings and operations. A store has to function. It has to make money. Its architecture has to be interesting and not just 'architecture for architecture's sake'. The danger we're seeing today is too many architects doing façades and regarding interiors as leftover spaces that need little attention. As a result, there's no connection between exterior and interior. They don't seem to understand the functional aspect of shopping. And when you have a building with five levels, like the Prada building in Tokyo, where each level is the same, no customer is going to walk up five floors. Do they even know what level they're on? Have they seen all five floors? Do they care? Why bother? They probably miss seeing 50 per cent of the floor area, which means half of the investment that Prada put into that building . . . The company lost a huge amount of money through its architectural decisions.

But are flagship stores like that one really built to sell products?

That's a good question. Are they made to sell? My answer is that they should be made to sell and that they should be good; architecture can do both. Our Omotesando store is extremely successful. It makes millions of dollars a month and it represents an excellent architectural solution. As for Prada in New York, it's got a lot of inspiration, but it doesn't make money. If I were the client, I would be quite upset, because the projection of an image is not enough. But it's not always the architect's fault. Fashion plays a part, too. If the products aren't interesting they won't sell, no matter how good the store is. People tend to blame the architect, but it's more complicated than just architecture.

Pfunds Molkerei
1891
Unknown architect, tiles by Villeroy & Boch
Bautzner Strasse 79, Dresden, Germany
(DESIGNER/CLIENT) (DISPLAY)
(MATERIALS) (SALES)

01 interior, general view

In 1880, Paul Gustav Leander Pfund (1849–1923) founded the dairy firm Dresdner Molkerei Gebrüder Pfund. Being the first in Germany to produce condensed milk, milk soaps and to develop high-quality food for infants, it quickly became a successful commercial empire. Pfund supplied Dresden and the world, but his greatest merit was the radical transformation in the way milk was produced and distributed and the initiation of new techniques, such as durable pasteurization (which he

DESIGNER/CLIENT introduced as early as 1900).

A representative building was built in 1891 on Bautzner Strasse in Dresden; it had office rooms and a café upstairs, as well as a milk bar and a shop downstairs. This dairy shop was the final element in a far-sighted philanthropic strategy: besides technological innovations and the control over the whole production and distribution process (from cow milking to drivers' uniforms), Paul Pfund also developed social programmes for his workers' welfare, sustaining them with housing and entertainment.

66 Pfunds Molkerei, Dresden (1891)

Because of new economic laws implemented by the German Democratic Republic, the company was fully nationalized in 1972. The shop interior was transformed – wall and floor tiles were removed to fulfil 'modernization measures'. After Pfund's heirs recovered the shop in 1990, it underwent a thorough restoration, and is now one of Dresden's main tourist attractions.

This shop originally sold the whole range of dairy products available, from milk to soaps, but the main product was always cheese. It was displayed on a massive counter topped with granite (70 cm high), or kept cool in a richly decorated refrigerator behind the counter, along the back wall. These two elements defined the realm of the salesperson, who thus had direct access to the cheese area, while the customer was separated from the products by glass **DISPLAY** screens. The cash desk was located to one side of the counter. On the other side, milk seemed to well out of the wall (this was actually a water fountain).

Economic transformations gradually led Pfund to diversify the range of products offered, by proposing cheese-related wines and delicacies. These products are mostly concentrated along the shop window, not on built-in displays in the shop but on mobile shelves added later (the shelves, however, blend into the richly decorated room).

02 façade

67 Pfunds Molkerei, Dresden (1891)

03 interior, detail of the
stairs

04 interior, café

68 Pfunds Molkerei, Dresden (1891)

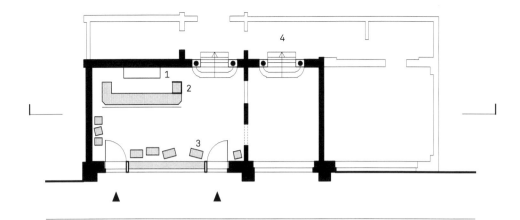

1. refrigerator   3. free-standing display
2. counter   4. access to the café upstairs

05 interior, plan

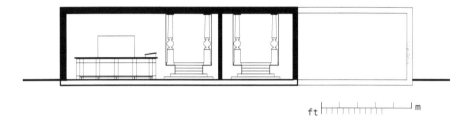

ft |‑‑‑‑‑‑‑‑‑‑‑| m

06 interior, section

The entire shop is covered with ceramic tiles, used for both their hygienic and decorative qualities. Paul Pfund's conceptions of hygiene and health were characteristic of the growing awareness for these matters at the beginning of the twentieth century. They met the specific requirements for sale and conservation of dairy products. The smooth tiled surface made the regular intensive cleaning of display elements and refrigerator easier. A white-glazed finishing, as traditionally used in the food industry, would have made the shop almost clinical; instead, 248 m^2 (2670 sq. ft) of hand-painted tiles (made by Villeroy & Boch and designed by Dresden artists) adorn walls,

MATERIALS panelled ceilings, furniture and candelabra-like columns. They depict picturesque Dutch landscapes with grazing cows, colourful ribbons of flowers and vine leaves, winged cherubs holding onto graduated cylinders and milk cans, and even a portrait of the German Kaiser and the English and American coat of arms. Gilded mirrors at both extremities of the shop expand the actual space and reflect the chandeliers located in the middle of the ceiling. Brass pipes protect the counter and the shop window from accidents. The result is a profusion of experiences and information, borrowed from German mannerist Renaissance. All this evokes a characteristic imagery, where Pfund products are depicted as both natural and highly technical.

69 Pfunds Molkerei, Dresden (1891)

During the renovation in 1995, Villeroy & Boch restored damaged tiles and the entire floor surface.

This renovation radically transformed the nature of the quiet dairy shop, and the current development of mass tourism has turned it into a tourist attraction, identified in 1997 as 'the most beautiful dairy store in the world' by the *Guinness Book of Records*. The original milk bar has been refurbished, and the small café upstairs became a 90-seat

SALES tasting room. The owners took advantage of the unique design of the shop to attract a mixed clientele of locals and thousands of weekly visitors. What was originally conceived of as a clever answer to hygienic issues is now considered to be a beautiful, slightly odd interior. It is this interior that is actually sold nowadays: the dairy products have become souvenirs, unable to compete with the appeal of the built environment and its economic potential.

Sources:

Gräfin Brühl, C., *Pfunds Molkerei*, Berlin: Kai Homilius Verlag, 1999

Stüting, M., *Der schönste Milchladen der Welt. Dresdner Molkerei Gebrüder Pfund*, Dresden: UDD, 1997

www.pfunds.de

Kniže
1905–13
Adolf Loos
Graben 13, Vienna, Austria
(DESIGNER/CLIENT) (MATERIALS)
(COMMUNICATION) (SOCIAL ISSUES)

01 interior, first floor: first salon

DESIGNER/CLIENT

A respected architect, Adolf Loos is particularly known for his writings, in which he tried to define modernity. His proposals tended to free architecture not so much of ornament (as his 1908 'Ornament and Crime' might suggest), but of its attachment – regardless of the economic and historical developments the period was facing – to stylistic conventions. In this respect, retail architecture was of prime importance to him, as it is there that economic developments take place and are given physical representation. He understood the cultural role that such architecture plays in the urban environment: in his magazine article *Das Andere*, published in 1903, he called, for instance, for the 'last Viennese portal of Old Vienna' (the eighteenth-century-style portal of the Exinger Company) to be transferred to the municipal museum.

72 Kniže, Vienna (1905–13)

It is no surprise that Loos was considered a very competent designer of shop interiors, building thirty of them throughout his career. In 1905, Fritz Wolff, a tailor appointed by the Austrian-Hungarian court, asked him to design several shops for his Kniže Company. The first, located on prominent Graben Boulevard, served as an example for other shops completed in Berlin and Paris.

Loos' use of traditional materials (wood, stone, brass and glass), his truthfulness to their very nature and intrinsic qualities, combined with the absence of ornamentation, corresponded to the statements he exposed in his numerous writings. Both in space and in materialization, the Kniže shop design followed these rules:

MATERIALS mirrors were placed in strategic places (on the ground floor, above doors, in staircases) to make spaces appear larger than they were. Walls, ceilings and floor (wood panelling, stucco, carpet flooring) showed Loos' preference for simple elegance; they formed a quiet, almost neutral background for the retail elements and activity.

facing page
02 interior, ground floor

73 Kniže, Vienna (1905–13)

04 interior, first floor:
second salon, where the suits
were fitted

Wooden built-in cupboards and glazed showcases ensured the
correct and efficient display of wares. All other supportive functions
(the paying area, storage or accesses to the dressing rooms, atelier
and office) were integrated into the built-in furniture system. This
showed Loos' talent for crafting an interior removed from existing
architectural constraints. But the range of materials also corresponded
to the expectations of the Kniže clientele. While department stores
transformed retail and initiated a new way for women to shop, this
salon addressed a masculine clientele, and therefore naturally
proposed a conventional interior. The result was quite representative
of Loos' ambiguous position, simultaneously modern and traditional –
modernity having to accommodate the nineteenth-century class
and gender distinctions.

    The entrance was designed to fulfil several goals. The general
symmetry, the use of dark granite for the portal and the minimalist
structure of shop windows and front door gave the shop the classical
COMMUNICATION allure befitting a tailor's clientele. But the interrelation and detailing
of these elements also created a subtle triggering effect. The granite
pillars curved inward to large shop windows, allowing a clear view of
the goods. These, however, were recessed into the façade, while the
stone base on which they stood was not. The client, not able to

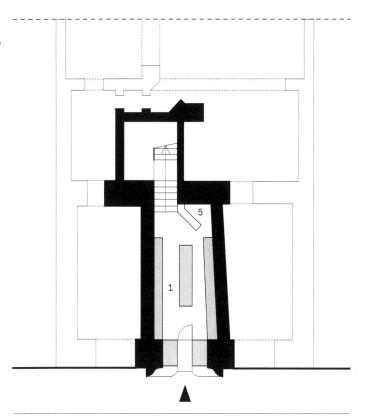

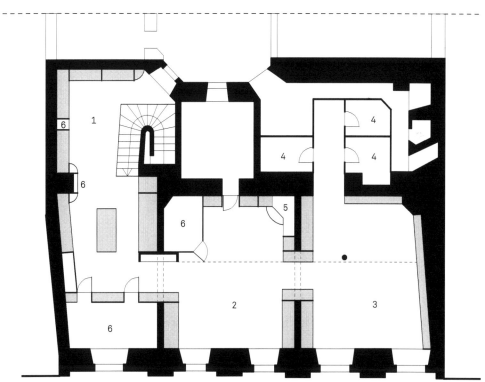

1. apparels and accessories   4. dressing room
2. first salon   5. cash desk
3. second salon   6. storage

on mezzanine: ateliers

approach the shop windows directly, therefore had to enter the narrow space between them in order to see more, a movement that brought him almost into the shop itself. This architectural trick functioned as a device to slowly attract and catch potential buyers.

The interior was such that it allowed a subtle filtering: while both floors shared the same fitting elements, they differed in the way that they addressed the double constraint of the product and of the clientele.

On the ground floor, items were sold that were available to a vast majority of customers (those who dared enter). These were basic commodities that did not need a particularly renewable display. Ranging from underwear to accessories, these goods were piled up and stacked in two lateral cupboards and a central showcase. The glazed furniture made a quick and efficient survey of all goods possible. The pay area at the rear allowed good visual control of the boutique. The strong symmetry of the ensemble echoed that of the façade.

SOCIAL ISSUES The upper floor, however, was strikingly different. It was reserved for tailor work, and an enfilade of rooms had the atmosphere of a men's club. Customers stayed here longer, and the range of display and furniture elements used was much larger than on the ground floor. To the standard mirrors and built-in cupboards, new devices were added that emphasized a domestic character: the way in which furniture – large leather armchairs, carpets and reading tables – was used and positioned, and conventionally carved ceiling patterns. Goods were displayed using techniques such as shelves and stacking, but puppets and small *mise en scènes* were also used. The design managed to make the two different activities of retailing and tailoring work complementary.

Sources:

Kristan, M., *Adolf Loos, Läden und Lokale*, Vienna: Album Verlag für Photographie, 2001

Sarnitz, A., *Loos*, Cologne: Taschen, 2003

Schezen, R., Frampton, K. and Rosa, J., *Adolf Loos: Architecture 1903–1932*, New York: Monacelli, 1996

Stewart, J., *Fashioning Vienna: Adolf Loos' Cultural Criticism*, London: Routledge, 2000

Tournikiotis, P., *Adolf Loos*, Princeton, NJ: Princeton Architectural Press, 1994

Bally shoe shop
1928
Robert Mallet-Stevens
11 boulevard de la Madeleine,
Paris, France
(DESIGNER/CLIENT) (COMMUNICATION)
(SOCIAL ISSUES) (MATERIALS)

01 façade

DESIGNER/CLIENT In 1928, the Swiss luxury shoe company Bally asked Robert Mallet-Stevens to refurbish a boutique in Paris, the first step in a strategy to open several new outlets in France. This was a deliberate choice: the French architect had already designed numerous commercial interiors (banks, kiosks, garages) and was well known in the 1920s fashion world. His interest in decorative arts meant that he regularly collaborated with artists and craftsmen, whose talent he used in almost every project. For the Bally shop, he worked with André Salomon, Hélène Henry and Louis Barillet, all famous industrial designers of their time. By 1937, Mallet-Stevens had built five other shops for the company, but this one remained the most famous.

77 Bally, Paris (1928)

02 detail of the shop window

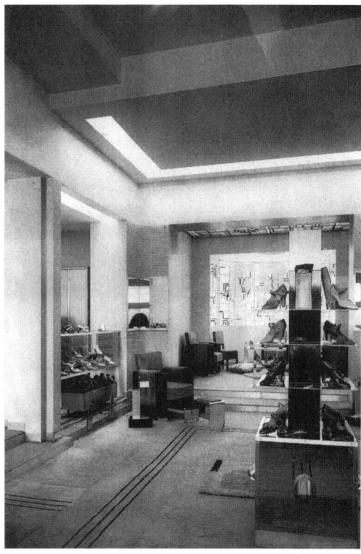

04 interior, general view

COMMUNICATION

The façade Mallet-Stevens designed offered a rather spectacular composition in the conservative Parisian 16th *arrondissement* (it was indeed judged scandalous and inappropriate when it opened). The only components were glass and plates of chromed nickel-silver, a hard, age-resistant alloy that imitates silver. The jointed plates were screwed on a metallic bearing structure, with screws left visible.

The architect created a rich interaction of volumes on several planes. The bronze entrance door on the left side was set back in the existing façade; a second layer was applied directly onto the existing building structure. A third was defined by elements jutting out: the plinth, the prominent door frame, the shop window and the shop sign, designed for close viewing in thin gold letters. Finally, the marquee, used as a lighting device (with lamps behind opaque glass plates), projected even further from the façade.

79 Bally, Paris (1928)

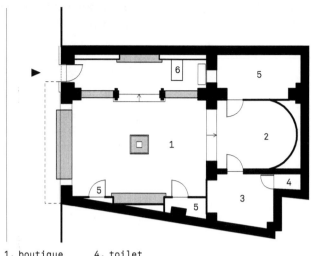

1. boutique   4. toilet
2. grand salon 5. storage
3. petit salon 6. cash desk

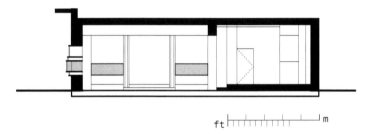

The long rectangular shop window displayed a small selection of shoes at eye level. The two glazed panels that bordered it also provided light to the interior. The result was a façade inviting customers in not so much by exhibiting products, but rather by enticing them with the promise of reserved luxury. The shop window and sign were so delicate and refined that they only revealed themselves to customers in close proximity, hence near to the entrance.

In order to avoid being closed for too long, the boutique was renovated in two stages. Also, Mallet-Stevens was not allowed to do any heavy structural transformation of the existing building but he managed to define specific spaces nonetheless. The entrance corridor

SOCIAL ISSUES led to the cash counter, clad in the same nickel-silver plates as used on the façade. The three retail spaces, called 'boutique', 'grand salon' and 'petit salon', were separated by steps, columns and/or showcases, and corresponded to the hierarchical organization that such a luxury shop implied. The deeper one went, the more exclusive the selling space became, the 'petit salon' being a distinct room for preferred customers.

80 Bally, Paris (1928)

In this sense, the shop followed the traditional division characteristic of boutiques of this period.

By placing displays to the sides, a free central space was cleared. Bally allowed customers to freely stroll around the room while trying on shoes and to glance at mirrors placed between display shelves. Storage was partly integrated in the shop, in two residual corners in the 'boutique' space (the main storage was probably located downstairs).

MATERIALS The counterpoint to the spectacular metallic exterior was a decorative interior: carpeted floors, paintings on white-plastered walls and built-in lighting in all the rooms. The 'grand salon' formed the backdrop of the shop and therefore offered a large range of luxurious finishings: a half-circular stained glass window backlit by 130 lamps, a 1.4 m-wide cupola, cushions on the floor on which to lay one's feet, a leafy shellac door. The 'petit salon' had wooden panelling, private toilets and a built-in elliptic reflector for lighting. All these elements were sophisticated and luxurious, contributing to the feeling of being in an extraordinary space. The façade and the interior differed in terms of atmosphere; yet both were designed according to decorative arts rules, a feature that provided unity.

Sources:

Cinqualbre, O., *Robert Mallet-Stevens, l'œuvre complete*, Paris: Editions du Centre Pompidou, 2005

Deshoulières, D. and Jeanneau, H., *Rob Mallet-Stevens architecte*, Brussels: Archive d'Architecture Moderne, 1980

Jacob, D., 'Le chausse-pied et l'architecte', *Faces 51*, 2002: 91–5

Grayson
1941
Victor Gruen and Elsie Krummeck
1514 Third Avenue, Seattle, USA
(DESIGNER/CLIENT) (SALES)
(COMMUNICATION) (MATERIALS)

82 Grayson, Seattle (1941)

02 view from the outside
towards the sunken
shop window

DESIGNER/CLIENT

Austrian-born architect Victor Gruen (1903–80) emigrated to the United States in 1938, and is generally considered to be the inventor of the shopping mall. He developed the concept throughout his career, first at the invitation of *Architectural Forum* in 1943. This typology quickly became central to his practice, and he and his wife Elsie Krummeck designed numerous projects, among them the large department store for Milliron in 1947 and Dayton's Southdale Mall in Minneapolis in 1956.

Gruen's initial involvement in retail design was forced upon him by necessity: the Depression of the 1930s forced him to go looking for commissions in this specific field of architecture, a historically despised activity. He started his work in the United States by designing a couple of boutiques on Fifth Avenue in New York. His career took a decisive step when Grayson, a chain selling low-priced apparel and accessories for women, asked him and Krummeck to come up with a new shop design. Between 1940 and 1947, they designed or remodelled twelve shops for this fast-growing company.

83 Grayson, Seattle (1941)

03 interior, sunken
shop window

04 interior, general view

84 Grayson, Seattle (1941)

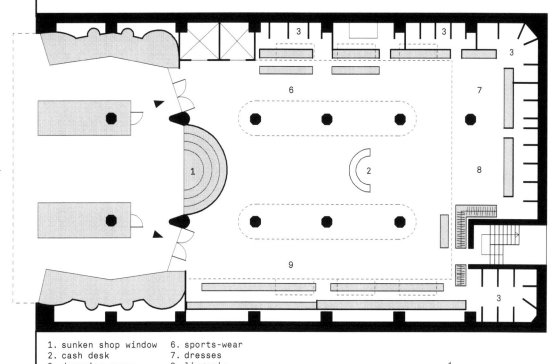

1. sunken shop window   6. sports-wear
2. cash desk   7. dresses
3. dressing rooms   8. lingerie
4. niche display   9. hoisery
5. storage

05 plan
06 section

85 Grayson, Seattle (1941)

This cooperation proved to be positive for both parties: Gruen launched his career as a retail specialist and Grayson set standards in development strategy that were soon applied by most chain stores. Although these standards were criticized by a number of real estate and retail executives at the time, Grayson's growth was both impressive and fast.

Grayson was actually responding to the transformations that the Second World War brought to American society. This new model of retail organization was later applied in Europe, as well. This shop epitomized the advent of mass culture and mass market. Wartime had given women financial independence, and the market that catered to them was the fastest growing retail sector. By offering a vast range of **SALES** cheap products, by adapting opening hours to working hours and by introducing theatrical elements into the design, Grayson not only allowed the growing middle class to go shopping, but also turned shopping into a social and entertaining activity. By offering nationwide stores with a common design language, it mirrored the new, more mobile market, strengthening the bond throughout the country and creating a feeling of familiarity in America's main streets.

Gruen and Krummeck brought some retail techniques to the downtown areas of American cities that were developed in suburban, strip-scale architecture. They employed a vocabulary usually applied in cinemas and theatres, and turned the façade into a monumental device that attracted both pedestrians and the new consumers of 1950s American society: car shoppers.

A complex shop-window system pulled the shop out of its actual premises, projecting it into the public sphere of the street, where it was able to 'trap' passers-by. Made up of two show islands and two show windows, with a floor that slowly sloped from the shop to the pavement, it created an intermediate zone that eliminated the idea of **COMMUNICATION** an entrance threshold. Here, the private space of the shop and the public space of the pavement meet.

The amount of display surface obtained by such an organization is large and multifaceted. One particular device was the indoor sunken amphitheatre along the façade: it offered various display possibilities, without obstructing the view to the inside. In order to attract car shoppers, the façade was scaled up: a three-storey high cement-plastered vault flanked by two travertine-clad walls, with the company name at the top. Free-standing lettering and dramatically lit columns reinforced this effect from a distance.

Gruen and Krummeck took advantage of the development of scientific research on lighting and could demonstrate the perfect compatibility of traditional (incandescent) and new (fluorescent) lighting. New fluorescents diffused a whiter light that can easily be used as basic lighting. In Grayson, fluorescents were concealed under columns capitals and in wall niches and shadow boxes. They provided a sufficient lighting level in the shop and a more dramatic, theatrical atmosphere at the same time. Incandescent light proved of limited

86 Grayson, Seattle (1941)

efficiency as basic lighting (small range, shadow casting), but was excellent for creating targeted spotlights on goods and display elements.

The new lighting techniques had an influence on display. The range and variety of products sold induced a wide range of techniques: hanging clothes in recessed niches, cupboard walls, **MATERIALS** desks, and small display tables. The combination of these diverse elements, the controlled use of light and a neutral background (plastered walls) created an environment of great refinement and clearness, in which the orientation of the clientele is optimal. This was reinforced by the large area of the shop, allowing potential clients to freely stroll around.

Sources:

Hardwick, J. M., *Mall Maker: Victor Gruen, Architect of an American Dream*, Philadelphia, PA: University of Pennsylvania Press, 2004

Nicholson, E., *Contemporary Shops in the United States*, New York: Architectural Book Publishing Company, 1945

Parnes, L., *Planning Stores That Pay: Organic Design and Layout for Efficient Merchandising*, New York: Dodge, 1948

Olivetti showroom, 1954
Studio BBPR
(Gian Luigi Banfi, Lodovico B.
Belgiojoso, Enrico Peressutti,
Ernesto N. Rogers)
580 Fifth Avenue, New York, USA
(DESIGNER/CLIENT) (DISPLAY)
(MATERIALS)

01 view from the outside   **88 Olivetti, New York (1954)**

Camillo Olivetti founded the first Italian typewriter factory in 1908 in Ivrea; later on, his company moved towards producing teleprinters, calculators, office furniture and fittings during the 1930s and 1940s. By the 1950s, it had established itself as the undisputed leader in mechanical office products, and combined this technological excellence with a strong focus on the market and a keen interest in design. Olivetti epitomizes the creativity in post-war Italian industrial design.

DESIGNER/CLIENT Olivetti commissioned the Italian studio BBPR (founded in 1932) to build its first showroom in the United States. Despite realizing only a limited number of buildings, BBPR had a major impact on the theoretic field, influencing generations of architects through their activities as university teachers (Belgiojoso, Peressutti, Rogers) and editor (Rogers at *Casabella*). Their work (especially the Velasca tower in Milan, 1958) was also often mentioned in the debate on Neoliberty that hit the world of Italian design in the late 1950s. Derived from Stile Liberty – also known as Art Nouveau – and defined by critic

02 exterior display with people

89 Olivetti, New York (1954)

03 interior, general view

90 Olivetti, New York (1954)

1
R. Banham, 'Neoliberty: The Italian Retreat from Modern Architecture', *Architectural Review* 747, 1959: 230–55

2
E.N. Rogers, 'Modern Architecture Since the Generation of the Masters' (trans.), *Casabella Continuità* 211, 1956: vii

3
S. Casciani, *L'architettura presa per mano*, Milan: Idea Books, 1992

Reyner Banham as 'the Italian retreat from modern architecture',[1] this movement departed from orthodox rationalism and proposed to go beyond, by forsaking the avant-garde and concentrating on continuity instead.[2] 'The BBPR group has brilliantly cut the ideological and formal rigour of modernism down to size: standard is not necessarily synonymous with geometry.'[3] Indeed, their work for Olivetti bore traces of this renewed interest for materials, ornamentation and crafts, while staying true to modernist values such as standardization. The Olivetti showroom on New York's Fifth Avenue opened in 1954 and closed in 1970.

Typewriters are a type of product directed at a specific clientele. Olivetti used its showroom for two purposes: as the market leader, to illustrate its machines' refinement and invention. It also served to re-place the company on a broader scale: with the Italian economy entering a period of unprecedented growth in the post-war period, and its industrial design growing incredibly successful, 'Italian-ness' became a relevant factor, economically speaking.

DISPLAY   The clear division of space corresponded to the selling process of such products. The showroom on the ground floor comprised typewriters displayed on various devices (spread throughout the space in a rather instinctual way), a reception desk for guidance and assistance, and a wall rack filled with take-home information cards. Upstairs on the mezzanine was an office space where business deals could be closed privately, which also functioned as a place where the

right
04 display element, lighting, wall

below
05 display element, section

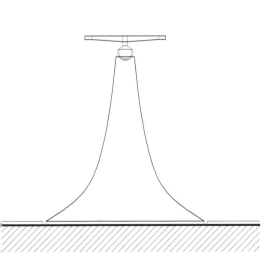

91 Olivetti, New York (1954)

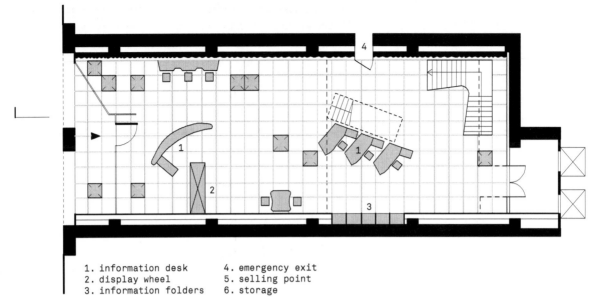

1. information desk   4. emergency exit
2. display wheel   5. selling point
3. information folders 6. storage

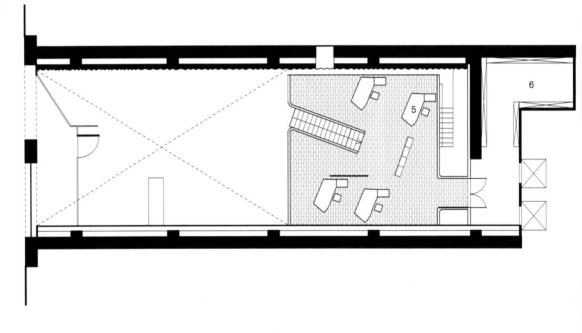

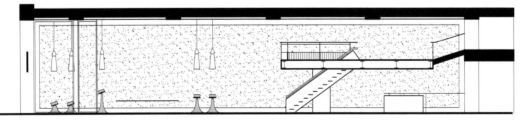

06 ground floor, plan
07 first floor, plan
08 interior, section

92 Olivetti, New York (1954)

machines and furniture (desks, foldable screens) were put *in situ*. Ergonomics and performance in an office environment were made directly visible to the customer.

All display devices were spectacular and participated in the evocation of Italian elegance and craftsmanship. They were singular elements, each suggesting a different world: a large brass wheel (echoing ones seen on Leonardo da Vinci's drawings?) brought typewriters in and out of the basement storage in a continuous movement; the demonstration tables were modular office desks. The most forthcoming display elements were pedestals that blended with the flooring; monolithic marble blocks of different heights. They turned machines into individual items to be tried out throughout the space, lit by individual hanging lamps.

The floor and its excrescences unified the space and brought inside and outside into dialogue: indeed, one pedestal, located beyond the formal entrance (glazed windows and a wooden door, all full height, around 5 m), allowed passers-by to test a typewriter on the street. For such a specific product, this was not as much about luring possible clients into the shop as it was about showing the company creativity – by placing a simple attraction in public space.

In order to create the Italian flair necessary for Olivetti, and according to BBPR's interest in Neoliberty, the architects had selected solely Italian materials and finishings: green Challant marble for the flooring, pink Candoglia marble for table boards and stair steps. The use of earth reds, ochres and pinks reinforced the Mediterranean aura. Furniture followed the same rules, with a series of lamps from Venini and office desks designed by BBPR itself. Those elements and materials

MATERIALS were made use of in a sophisticated but consequent way, and were produced according to the latest standardization processes (the ceiling seems to have been the only element not to have profited from innovative research). One lateral wall was plastered and had concealed lighting at its bottom and top; the main focus point of the shop, however, was the other longitudinal wall: artist Costantino Nivola decorated it with a wall relief, about 23 x 4.5 m in size. This low-relief frieze, made of aggregated sand (also produced with innovative casting techniques), combined formal and iconic figuration.

Sources:

'A Positive Example of Public Relations: The Olivetti Store in New York', *Technica ed Organizzazione*, 19, 1955

Fallan, K., *Shaping Sense, Italian Post-War Functionalistic Design* (2001), Online. Available www.hf.ntnu.no/itk/ikon/tekster/sense/index.php (accessed 24 March 2006)

Mumford, L., 'The Sky Line. Charivari and Confetti', *The New Yorker*, 8 December 1954

Ponti, G., 'Italia a New York', *Domus*, 298, 1954: 3–10

Watson Jr, T.J., 'Good Design is Good Business', in Schutte, T. (ed.) *The Art of Design Management*, New York: Tiffany, 1975

Retti candle shop
1965
Hans Hollein
Kohlmarkt 10, Vienna, Austria
(DESIGNER/CLIENT)
(COMMUNICATION) (MATERIALS)

01 interior, display niches
and mirror

94 Retti, Vienna (1965)

02 interior, looking back to
the entrance door

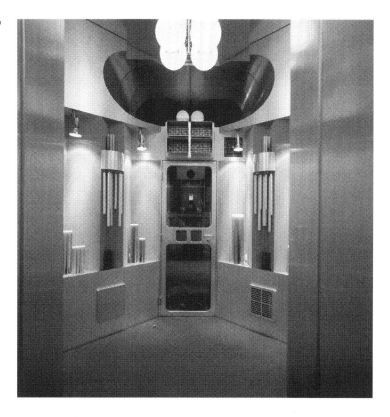

03 façade

95 Retti, Vienna (1965)

Today for the first time in the history of mankind, at this moment when immensely developed science and perfected technology offer the means, we are building what we want, making an architecture that is not determined by technique, but that uses technique – pure, absolute architecture.[1]

1
H. Hollein, 'Architecture', arts & architecture, August 1963, trans. K. Rheinfurt

DESIGNER/CLIENT

This statement perfectly defines the shop that Hans Hollein designed for candle-maker Marius Retti. It is one of first built projects by Hollein, who until then was better known for his theoretical works.

The brief was complex: to fulfil the functional requirements and to provide a maximum of space for a shop of only 14.8 m^2, while at the same time expressing elegance, extravagance and exclusivity (not least for sales-psychology reasons). This project allowed the architect to apply his concepts in reality, and as well as bringing Hollein international recognition, it won the R.S. Reynolds Memorial Award, presented by the American Institute of Architects, in 1966.

Kohlmarkt is an expensive location in the centre of the city, with neo-classical and baroque architecture. The whole character and attitude of this distinguished location had to be taken into account. Hollein found a contrasting solution, true to his architectural statements (on modernity and history) and his techniques (photomontage): radically different from the existing premises and fiercely modern, yet echoing the decorative elements present on neighbouring façades. The result is an aluminium-plated façade with as main feature a doorway whose form (two 'R's, back to back) alludes to

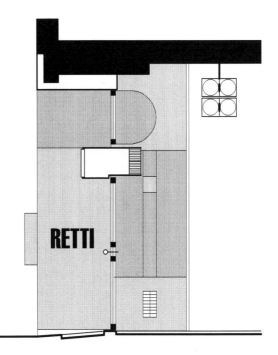

04 façade, section

96 Retti, Vienna (1965)

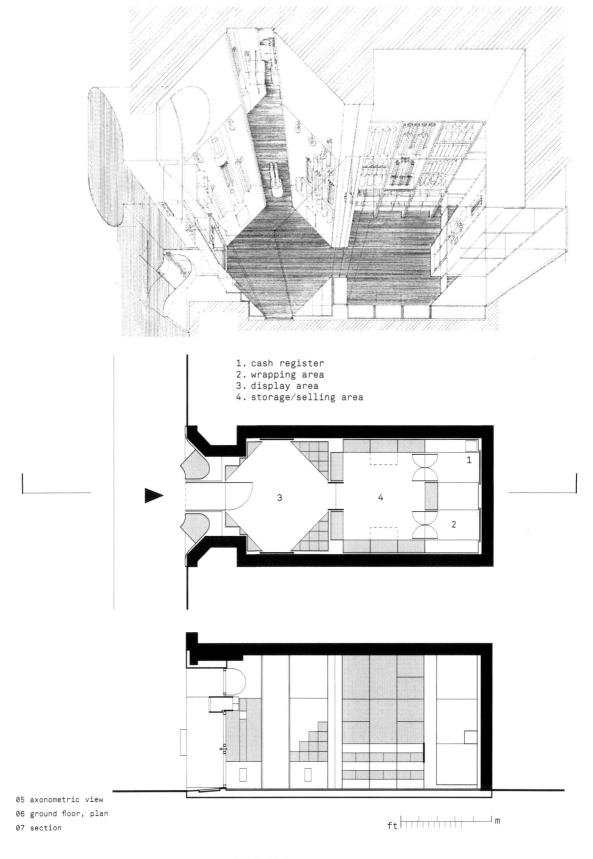

1. cash register
2. wrapping area
3. display area
4. storage/selling area

05 axonometric view
06 ground floor, plan
07 section

97 Retti, Vienna (1965)

the name of the owner. It also responds to the existing pillar above the shop. The plain façade functions on two levels: from a distance, the overall form takes over; up close, the small shop windows are directed towards the passer-by – and they are so small that they hinder the presence of more than one observer at a time. Attention is not drawn to the shop by neon signs or such: architecture plays this role, supported by curiosity.

COMMUNICATION The narrow shop windows illustrate the absence of a need for advertisement, as this product cannot really be advertised, and it is not really about impulsive shopping here.

The interior follows the same idea, with a strong subdivision of space from front to back: closed shop windows, an octagonal area where nothing is sold but everything displayed, a selling/storage area and, finally, the paying and wrapping zone. All these spaces are separated from each other by narrow thresholds.

In Retti, architecture does not describe the product, the interior solely evokes an environment, a certain holiness of place that expresses the world the product is supposed to bring to mind: one of peace and interiorization.

Implementing the *Gesamtkunstwerk* ('synthesis of the arts') promoted by other Viennese architects such as Hoffmann, Hollein designed most of the elements in the shop himself, except for the technical equipment, which nevertheless was integrated into the overall scheme.

The extremely small size of the shop rendered the use of mirrors almost mandatory. By combining them with other components, a rather small space is transformed into an infinite, abstract world:

MATERIALS mirrors on both sides of the first room, the continuation of material (outside and inside are linked as aluminium flows from one to the other) and the thresholds that compress and extend the environment.

The main material used here is polished aluminium, anodized in its natural state. The outside plates have been glued on with epoxy, inside, the plates are screwed onto the surfaces. Chrome-plated steel adorns the display elements, together with orange shantung, which was used on the inside of display niches. All storage containers are covered with Formica. All these materials, contemporary in the 1960s, reflect the spirit of the time and show the use of technique and high technicity, but combined with high-quality craftsmanship, a certain flair for luxury.

Sources:

Barnbeck, U., *Architekten – Hans Hollein*, Stuttgart: IRB, 1987

Jenks, C., *Architecture Today*, New York: Harry N. Abrams, Incorporated, 1982

Pettena, G., *Hans Hollein: Works 1960–1988*, Milan: Idea, 1988

www.hollein.com

Flos showroom
1968, 1976, 1984, 1990
Achille Castiglioni with Pier Giacomo
Castiglioni (1968), Paolo Ferrari
(1976, 1984) and Italo Lupi (1990)
Corso Monforte 9, Milan, Italy
(DESIGNER/CLIENT) (DISPLAY)
(SALES) (MATERIALS)

01 1990: display niches

Flos's Milan showroom is a good example of a long-lasting cooperation between a brand and a designer. Achille Castiglioni, though trained as an architect, started by designing several lamp fittings for the Italian company. Some of his products, such as Arco (1962), Parentesi (1971) and Frisbi (1978), have become bestsellers since then.

DESIGNER/CLIENT   In 1968, Castiglioni was commissioned to design Flos's first showroom in central Milan. The brief was rather complex, as the proposal had to solve display, management and standardization issues. The design had to allow customers to browse through the entire selection of lamps; it had to provide a continuously flexible environment; it had to show the specific identity and quality of each product; and it had to be able to be repeated in other retail points.

99 Flos, Milan (1968, 1976, 1984, 1990)

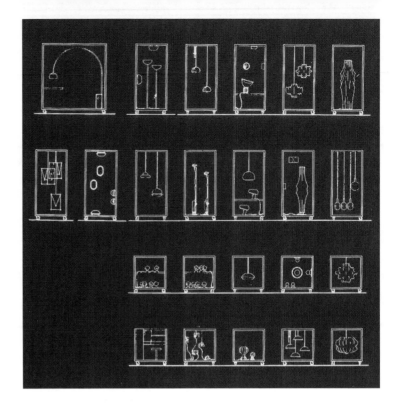

After the first design in 1968, Castiglioni went on to make three
more for the same space in Corso Monforte, in 1976, 1984 and 1990.
These changes were due to the necessity of regularly changing the
interior of the showroom and of adapting it to the flair of the day,
but also to practical requirements. The growing success of the
company implied an increase in production and thus a need for
more display space.

Castiglioni's knowledge of lamp fittings provided him with strong
positions on light, especially on the independence of artificial lighting
with regard to natural light, and on the fact that fittings must be
secondary to the quality of light itself.[1] These two points of view were
put into practice spatially in the showroom.

In the four successive designs, Castiglioni chose to use the specific
characteristics of the light produced by each fitting, and to use this as
the main light source for the shop.

The 1968, 1976 and 1984 plans functioned in a similar way: free-
standing showcases were spread against a background: both features,
rather neutral, allowed one to focus on the goods on display. These
DISPLAY were placed in/on independent movable cases and grouped according
SALES to type (ceiling or wall fittings, table lamps, etc.). Each container
worked as an insulation chamber, concentrating the customer's
attention on one specific type of product.

In 1968, the display cases were rectangular solids (either 1.6 or
2.2 m high) made out of white plastic laminate, and open on one side.

1
Castiglioni, A., 'Lighting
Introduction: Interview with
Raffaella Crespi', in *Design Since
1945*, Exhibition Catalogue,
Philadelphia, PA: Philadelphia
Museum of Art, 1983, p. 139–42

100 Flos, Milan (1968, 1976, 1984, 1990)

03 1976: display elements
04 1984: display elements
05 1990: central corridor

101 Flos, Milan (1968, 1976, 1984, 1990)

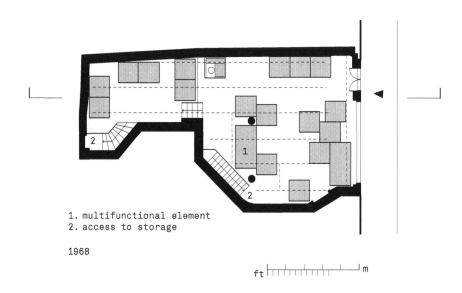

1. multifunctional element
2. access to storage

1968

ft ⊢⊢⊢⊢⊢⊢⊢⊢⊢ m

102 Flos, Milan (1968, 1976, 1984, 1990)

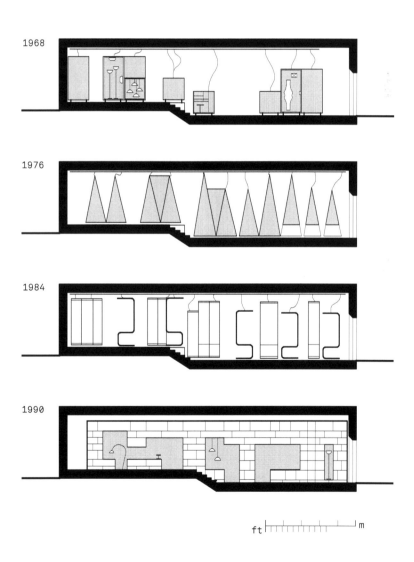

1. staff/cash register
2. access to storage

1990

1968

1976

1984

1990

ft ⌐———————┐ m

103 Flos, Milan (1968, 1976, 1984, 1990)

The office and information desk were also integrated into such cubic elements. They were all mounted on wheels for flexible use.

In 1976, Flos's success implied a larger range of products, and Castiglioni chose to use more compact trihedrons. He had already experimented with such trihedrons in his design for the 'Pesticides for Agriculture' room at the 33rd Milan Trade Fair in 1955, and would use them again in 1980 for the *Forum Design* exhibition in Linz. They were made out of an enamelled metal tubular structure with laminate shelves and dust-proof fabric. This design offered an improvement over the one from 1968: the trihedrons could be combined two by two, forming an inverted trihedron that could easily increase the display area if needed.

In 1984, lamps were hung from vertical 'S' or 'C'-shaped stands, made out of coloured plastic laminate. This material highlighted light elements; combined with their shape, it allowed even more combinations, larger display surfaces and specific settings. In these three designs, the presentation was focused on the products, whereas the rest of the space became an abstract environment.

A radical change occurred between the design from 1984 and that of 1990. By 1990, production had increased so dramatically that it proved impossible to simply increase the number of showcases in the 110 m² shop. Castiglioni chose a different concept in answer to these new givens: a simulation of real-life situations. With this display technique, the accent was no longer on the fittings as such, but on the atmosphere they participated in creating. For this purpose, Castiglioni designed a labyrinth-like space: a central inner road loops through the shop, and is bordered by dummy stone walls. Behind those walls is a series of small independent rooms, varying in size and shape and in which lamps are no longer grouped by type, but co-exist the way they usually do in interiors (in the kitchen, the living room, the bedroom and so forth). This form of display entailed a radical change in the way light was presented: and while this change had to do with some distribution constraints (the number of products to be displayed, for instance), it introduced a new way to exhibit, a *mise en scène* that has replaced the solo presentation in most showrooms. Here the quality of light produced by each fitting gives way to the one created by the interplay of different types.

Despite their differences, all four designs share some common supportive features. Conductive ducts mounted on the ceiling allowed the electricity supply to be flexible and facilitated the grouping of lighting fittings, and therefore the control of the exact concentration of light in the shop. As a counterpart to this, walls and ceilings have always been kept dark and matte throughout the years (with different materials, though: brown fabric in 1968 and grainy tan-coloured quartz **MATERIALS** ceramic in 1976, for instance). They acted as absorbers and neutralized any disruptive, uncontrolled light effect.

In the three first designs (1968, 1976 and 1984), the diversity in light effects and quality was achieved by the interplay of this neutral background with the display elements. Those were free-standing showcases that played different roles: they suppressed any interference between the different lighting systems; they reinforced the characteristics of each lamp. At the same time, they acted as sources of lighting for the entire shop. Moreover, these different displays were made out of materials highly reactive to light: shiny smooth material (plastic laminate) that reflects it, or, on the contrary, fabric that absorbs it and allows shadow effects.

In the 1990 design, separate rooms are defined by walls made of honeycomb panels with metallic paintwork. The interiors of these rooms were painted in a light colour, to enhance light diffusion.

Sources:

Casciani, S., 'A Milano per esporre delle lampade', *Domus*, 723, 1991: 64–7

Casciani, S., *Negozio Flos*, Barcelona: Atrium, 1992, p. 104–11

Castiglioni, A., 'Espositori alla Flos', *Ottagono*, 45, 1977: 48–9

Castiglioni, A., 'Lampade in vetrina', *Ottagono*, 76, 1985: 112–3

'Lampade sotto osservazione', *Domus*, 474, 1969: 35–7

Polano, S., *Achille Castiglioni: Complete Works*, Milan: Electa, 2001

105 Flos, Milan (1968, 1976, 1984, 1990)

**Let It Rock – Too Fast to Live Too
Young to Die – SEX – Seditionaries –
World's End
1971–80**
**Malcolm MacLaren and Vivienne
Westwood, Seditionaries designed
by Ben Kelly and David Connor
430 King's Road, London, UK**
(LOCATION) (DESIGNER/CLIENT)
(SOCIAL ISSUES) (MATERIALS)
(COMMUNICATION)

01 1974: 'SEX': interior with
Jordan and jukebox

1
Ben Kelly, London, October 2005

LOCATION

During the 1960s, the King's Road changed from a conventional High Street to one of the centres of creative activity in London. Historically an artists' area, Chelsea was an interesting mix of 'old money and no money':[1] gentrified properties, but also artists' ateliers, recordings studios, the Chelsea drugstore (with the Rolling Stones as regular visitors) and the Art Club around the corner. The King's Road acquired the role of a runway for bands, underground theatrical productions (*Look Back in Anger*, *The Rocky Horror Show*) and fashion designers like Mary Quant, Vivienne Westwood and Ossie Clark. Rents were cheap in this interesting setting, and the street turned into a perfect catalyst for young rebellious characters. This spirit was visible in the urban landscape, with a series of glamorous shops in which owners expressed their ideas about society.

02 1974: 'SEX': façade

In November 1971, Malcolm MacLaren and Vivienne Westwood rented the back half of a shop called 'Paradise Garage' to open a stall selling Teddy Boy clothes and 1950s records under the name 'Let It Rock'. Even though this style was not in fashion at the time, it proved successful within a few months. They took over the whole shop and went from being simple retailers to clothes designers.

In the spring of 1973, their interests shifted and they reopened the shop as 'Too Fast to Live Too Young to Die', a tribute to James Dean, where they sold clothes inspired by the rebellious spirit of bikers.

In April 1974, the shop took on a completely new face, 'SEX', adopting the S&M imagery and questioning the sexually repressed English society of that time. The most important step was Westwood creating the Sex Pistols' look, after the future members of the band, looking for a lead singer, met John Lydon, a.k.a. Johnny Rotten, in her shop.

'Seditionaries' in 1977 went a step further with the introduction in fashion of elements that would eventually define the punk look: ripped and militaristic clothing, razor blades, zippers and dog collars.

DESIGNER/CLIENT

In the autumn of 1980, with the release of Vivienne Westwood's new work, 430 King's Road went through another refit. A large clock, with a thirteen-hour face that ran backwards, was installed on the façade. The new shop, evoking the back of a galleon, was named after that part of King's Road: 'World's End'. This was the first shop fully inspired by Westwood's set of ideas, and is still one of her selling points today.

The numerous transformations the shop went through were fast and drastic; they were direct translations of MacLaren and Westwood's evolution and of ongoing social changes. Through these different avatars, they cleverly managed to address successive targets. Entering the shop did not necessarily mean buying something; it gave alternative groups a place to hang out, to meet similarly minded people and to express one's identity. Music played a central role.

SOCIAL ISSUES

Regular harassment by the police or the neighbouring Chelsea Football Club fans can be seen as a side effect of the social role the shop always played. It did indeed create shockwaves: influencing other shops, being in the press and eventually becoming a place of pilgrimage for people world-wide. Provocation had a double meaning: it was a natural way for MacLaren and Westwood to rebel against institutionalized order, but also to attract attention, and hence to be able to go on creating. Here, statement and publicity go hand in hand.

The two owners, with the help of friends or visitors to their shop, went to the unfashionable outer London markets to hunt for merchandise and items that would help create the imagined

MATERIALS environment: ornamental jars of Brylcreme and 1950s living room furniture for 'Let It Rock'; a 1950s jukebox and lines from Valerie Solanas's *S.C.U.M Manifesto* on 'SEX' walls; an upside-down picture of Piccadilly Circus and spotlights poking through holes in the ceiling for

03 1977:
'Seditionaries': interior

04 1977: 'Seditionaries':
sketch by David Conner

05 1977:
'Seditionaries': façade

the 'bombed out Dresden' concept of 'Seditionaries' . . . it was not so much about designing a space, but more about raising an atmosphere by using vintage elements charged with cultural connotations. And of course, cheap materials allowed changes to happen almost overnight.

In this search for constant rebellion and differentiation, the entrance and façade were critical. 'SEX' had huge pink padded plastic letters topping traditional shop windows painted white. Here, the intrinsic nature of the façade as a billboard was pushed to the simplest, most direct expression, with a single strong element enough to convey the message.

COMMUNICATION   The 'Seditionaries' façade took an opposite course to the rather exotic and loud surroundings of that time: white flashed opal glass, a neon light above the entrance door and an etched brass plaque

108 MacLaren and Westwood, London (1971–80)

06 1980: 'World's End': façade

reminiscent of that of a solicitor's office. This hybrid, almost minimal design had to be boarded up later on because of regular football fan attacks, and then spray-painting by punks.

As in the interior, the use of second-hand or mundane materials prevailed for the façade. A change happened from the 'World's End' period on, when flourishing business finally allowed a more sophisticated façade.

Sources:

Fogg, M., *Boutique: A '60s Cultural Phenomenon*, London: Mitchell Beazley, 2003

Gallix, A., *Only Anarchists Are Pretty, Interview with Andrew Wade*, Online. Available www.3ammagazine.com/litarchives/may2001_andrew_wade_interview.html (accessed 12 March 2006)

Mital, U., *Vivienne Swire/Vivienne Westwood*. Online. Available www.mital-u.ch/PunkWave/index.html (accessed 12 March 2006)

Wilcox, C., *Vivienne Westwood*, London: V&A Publications, 2004

www.only-anarchists.co.uk

Issey Miyake
1987
Shiro Kuramata
Seibu department store building B,
1F21-1 Utagawa-Mchi, Shibuya-ku,
Tokyo, Japan
(DESIGNER/CLIENT)
(MATERIALS) (LOCATION)

01 view from inside the mall

Shiro Kuramata (1934–91) was a driving force in Japanese design. Known for his use of reduced, uncommon materials, he started his practice in 1965 and soon combined the Japanese tradition of the unity of the arts with contemporary Western culture. Trained as an industrial designer, he always remained interested in industrial materials such as acrylic, glass, aluminium and steel mesh. Although these were uncommon materials to use in interior designs in Kuramata's time, he experimented with them in most of the 300 boutiques and restaurants he designed in his career.

DESIGNER/CLIENT

02 interior, general view
03 display, detail

Of his various clients, he shared a particular relationship with fashion designer Issey Miyake: after designing the boutique in the Bergdorf Goodman department store in New York in 1984, Kuramata built most of Miyake's boutiques until 1989. Their business relationship was supported by friendship and a common drive in search of a state of 'weightlessness'. This found its expression in Kuramata's attempt to capture the couturier's designing skills and to translate them into architecture. Ideally, shops should convey fashion techniques into architecture: superposition, texture contrasts or brilliance.

The design for the boutique in Seibu department store in Shibuyaku, Tokyo, was completed in 1987, one year after Kuramata launched the chair 'How High the Moon'. This chair was a clear source of inspiration. Named after a jazz piece by Duke Ellington, it is entirely made out of rib mesh, and the same material was used to turn the shop into an evocation of Miyake's fashion, built in metal. This type of material allowed Kuramata to express abstraction, immateriality and to play with shadows and light.

MATERIALS Apart from the floor (made of mixed gravel tiles), he only used metal openwork and aluminium. A series of fifteen lightweight metallic arches forms the skeleton of both the vaulted ceiling and partition walls. It is covered by metal meshing painted black, of two different types to create *moiré* effects. This overall element defines the space of the shop and encloses the other components: displays, pay desk, changing rooms and storage area. Each arch of the metallic vault hangs by three points from the ceiling. On the window side, the partition walls reach down to the floor; on the corridor side, they rest on chrome-plated columns.

Displays consist of metal openwork rods and shelves and tubular elements. The chrome-plated, flawless finishing of these shiny elements contrasts with the dark environment. The superposition of several layers of mesh either neutralizes the existing elements (windows) or incorporates them (the frame of the technical ceiling becomes like another, larger mesh), while at the same time isolating the shop from the rest of the department store. The general *moiré* effect is reinforced by light that has been incorporated between the existing ceiling and the vault.

The Miyake boutique is part of a conglomerate of different showrooms in Seibu department store, one of the largest at that time. It is a shop-in-a-shop, and this retail type differs quite frankly from classic street-front boutiques. Because of being in a department store, several physical constraints are absent, for instance, those of providing a waterproof shelter, a secure environment and independent facility **LOCATION** supplies. At the same time, other limitations, like the position of lighting and technical facilities, have to be dealt with. This environment also implies a stronger immediate competition, because of the high concentration of similar boutiques or because of the shopping mall environment; shops, therefore, have to distinguish themselves. These two factors entail a type of architecture deliberately

1. shelves
2. hanger pipes
3. cash desk
4. dressing rooms
5. storage

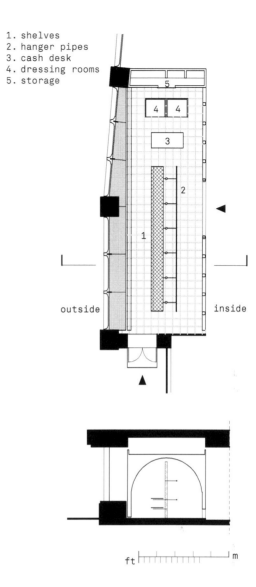

representational of a designer's world. One technique used was the denial of the existing surroundings. This design ignored the existing physical features of its location: a series of windows on one side and a technical ceiling. The flooring (stone tiles) is also radically different from that of the public space of the department store.

Source:

Fitoussi, B., *Showrooms*, Princeton, NJ: Princeton Architectural Press, 1990

113 Issey Miyake, Tokyo (1987)

Comme des Garçons SHIRT
1988
Rei Kawakubo, Yasuo Kondo,
Toshiko Mori
Manhattan Soho, New York, USA

Comme des Garçons
1998
Rei Kawakubo, Future Systems,
Takao Kawasaki
520 W 22nd Street, Chelsea,
New York, USA

Guerrilla stores
Since 2004
Rei Kawakubo
Berlin, Singapore, Cologne,
Reykjavik, Warsaw and Athens,
among others
(DESIGNER/CLIENT)
(COMMUNICATION) (LOCATION)
(DISPLAY)

01 Comme des Garçons SHIRT:
façade

1
On Wooster Street, designed with
Takao Kawasaki. The project is
described in B. Fitoussi,
Showrooms, Princeton, NJ:
Princeton Architectural Press,
1990, p. 94–7

In 1983, Japanese designer Rei Kawakubo opened her first American
boutique in New York,[1] where it quickly attracted attention for its
radical approach. Not a single piece of clothing was actually displayed
and the architecture was minimal and bare: a raw concrete box,
furnished with just a few pieces of steel furniture. At the time, such a
combination was completely new for retail, and this shop started the
long line of innovative designs Kawakubo produced for her brand.

DESIGNER/CLIENT   The designer is a driving force in Japanese fashion, and she
sponsors up-and-coming artists and designers. By collaborating with
them, she constantly has new ideas at her disposal and manages to
regenerate her brand tirelessly. While she regularly works with
established architects (for instance, Takao Kawasaki and Future
Systems), she always involves young talent. Sometimes, designers work
separately on the same project, without being aware of the others'
proposals. Such a creative emulation provides Kawakubo with a large
amount of information that she herself organizes into a final design.
Her role can be described as that of a curator. The shop in Chelsea is a

good example of such teamwork, where Future Systems took care of
the entrance tunnel while Takao Kawasaki designed the interior.

Since 1983, what Kawakubo seems to propose is a constant anti-
shop, always resisting mainstream trends by systematically choosing
the opposite direction. Perhaps this is the sign of an avant-garde
outlook – it is certainly a clever retailing technique. In fact, she
understood the possibilities that retail could offer early on, before
fashion became the competitive market that it is. While brands and
their media exposure have multiplied (through advertisement or
sponsoring), she has managed to redefine what luxury is, and uses
architecture to do so, by making her outlets more than mere selling
points. As for other brands, her shops do provide a setting that refers
to socio-cultural connotations. But while these usually take the form of
specific materials or a typical division of space, Kawakubo is looking for
an overall feeling. Her shops are better conceived of as experience halls;

115 Comme des Garçons, New York (1988, 1998)

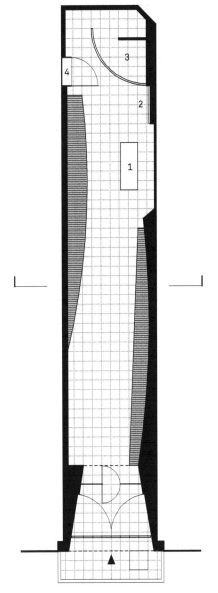

05 Comme des Garçons
SHIRT: interior

1. cash desk
2. mirror
3. dressing room
4. access to storage
   and staff room

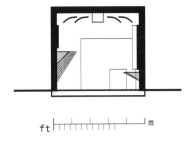

03 Comme des Garçons SHIRT: plan
04 Comme des Garçons SHIRT: section

they do not provide a background for brand merchandising, but are rather part of the brand itself. Product and shops are thus strongly bound, sometimes literally, with, for instance, limited-edition leather ware, with colours that recall the shop they are sold in: blue for Tokyo, red for Paris and green for New York.

116 Comme des Garçons, New York (1988, 1998)

The three shops presented here, while designed in different periods and under varying conditions, are characteristic of this ongoing investigation. By blurring architecture and fashion, Kawakubo creates a unique combination that allows her to relocate products from the sphere of commerce into the cultural field, and therefore to give them an added value. This strategy finds another means of expression in the recurrent use of art. At first this was conveyed through architecture itself, for instance in the early minimalism of Comme des Garçons SHIRT in New York. But by the end of the 1990s, pieces of art became part of the shop as such: in 2002 in Paris, studio KRD proposed a red gallery in front of the entrance, with red cubes slowly moving across the floor. The 2005 refurbishment of the Aoyama shop in Tokyo was done in cooperation with Belgian artist, Jan de Cock. The Dover Street Market in London, a luxury bazaar that opened in 2004, inspired by the late Kensington Market, can even be described as an art exhibition. Its raw interior consists of constructive elements and ducts left exposed, in which carefully selected designers were invited to each arrange a specified zone. Such designs ensure that these shops are published in media that address a possible target for Comme des

COMMUNICATION Garçons's products. They provide invisible, possibly unplanned, but certainly effective publicity.

There is a downside and a limit to this action, however: the influence these designs have on other brands limits their own durability and accurateness in time. Mainstream companies look at businesses like Comme des Garçons to feed their own inspiration. For instance, the shop and graphic design of brands such as The Gap, Mango or Zara clearly show some influences from other, more luxurious brands (Calvin Klein, Chloé and Prada, respectively).[2] Kawakubo's influence can be felt in the massive use of art in retail (a technique that has somehow become a classic by now), the qualification of fashion as a cultural artefact and, as a consequence of this process, in the appearance of concept stores.

When design is not enough to keep the lead, the choice of location can provide another escape. In the case of Kawakubo's boutiques, it is a good witness of the evolution in her understanding of what retail means.

Older shops were located in prime locations, like Omotesando Avenue in Tokyo or Soho, New York. Located on a narrow lot, Comme des Garçons SHIRT in Soho had a striking façade (a white plastered entrance) coming up onto the street. Such an architectural device created a threshold into the shop and other elements that could extend the distance to the public domain, such as security fences, were kept visible.

2
Top segment brands also benefit from this exchange: mainstream companies are dressing potential luxury customers that, in turn, inevitably pay a visit to the original

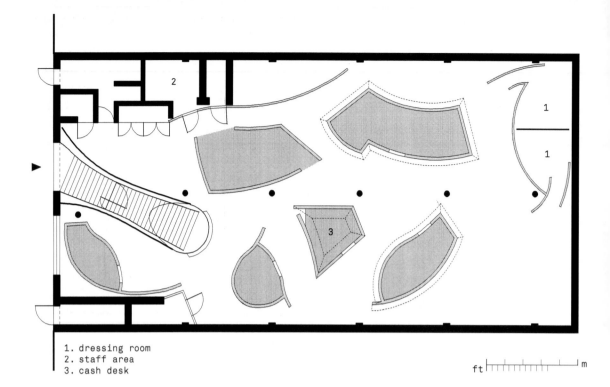

1. dressing room
2. staff area
3. cash desk

ft └─┴─┴─┴─┴─┴─┴─┴─┴─┘ m

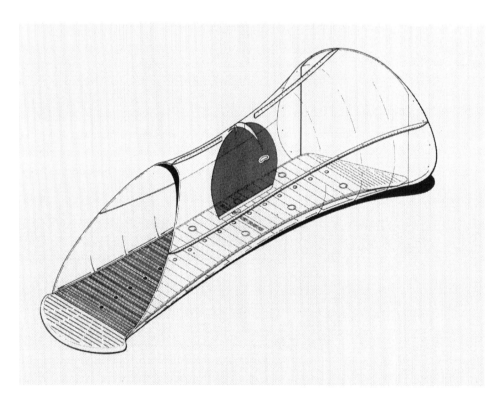

06 Comme des Garçons in New
York: plan

07 Comme des Garçons in New
York: tunnel, axonometry

118 **Comme des Garçons, New York (1988, 1998)**

08 Comme des Garçons in New
York: façade

09 Comme des Garçons in New
York: tunnel, detail

3
New York Times Magazine, 14
March 1999, *The New Yorker*,
8 March, 23 August and 30
August 1999, mentioned in
S. Zukin, Point of Purchase:
*The Transformation of Shopping
into Public Culture*, London:
Routledge, 2003, p. 208

4
The founders of the brand
Go Vacant claim to be the
initiator of this technique:
see www.govacant.com

For the Comme des Garçons shop opened in 1998, situated in
an old garage, she elected the Chelsea district, a part of the city off
the traditional fashion roads, but in the vicinity of some art galleries.
The existing situation and street frontage have been maintained to
LOCATION keep the traditional atmosphere. The choice of this location, and the
invisible, not outspoken, façade, help to blend the shop into an
environment that suits Kawakubo's idea of what her brand stands
for (eventually, this shop was named four times in the press as
an art venue).[3]

The same process is taken a step further with the so-called
Guerrilla stores. Opened for a period of just one year, they are situated
in neglected or non-commercial areas. The Berlin shop, presented here,
is located in an old bookshop on a large avenue in the eastern part of
the city. The technique of temporary outlets[4] is reminiscent of
squatting movements; it helps stage the brand in a different setting
than usual. Opposed to traditional advertising, a technique of
concealment is at play here that makes use of the customer's curiosity:
people have to look for these off-centre shops.

Business-wise, it is a perfect way to test new locations and to start
doing business in countries traditionally less fashionable, but where
there is interest from clients. And while Guerrilla shops are meant to
be open one year only, an exception was made in Berlin, as the city
proved to be a good market (when the shop closed down, another one
was opened in a different location).

119 Comme des Garçons, New York (1988, 1998)

10 Guerrilla store in
Berlin: façade

11 Guerrilla store in
Berlin: interior, detail
of the display

12 Guerrilla store
in Berlin: interior,
general view

The use of specific locations as a way to create distance or discretion seems to prevail today over earlier techniques such as concealed or closed façades (present in the older shops in Tokyo, Paris or Paris for Perfumes). An interesting phenomenon is the fact that these peculiar shops actually upgraded the district they were operating in, eventually turning them into a fashionable area and attracting retail activity.[5]

Another way to filter attention and to provoke curiosity and exclusivity is through display. For her line of Comme des Garçons

5
Using the same technique of temporary shops, the Dutch magazine Blend was asked in 2006 to open an outlet in Groningen, in order to revitalize a neglected area of the city

SHIRT shops, even though intended for a slightly less exclusive market, Kawakubo chose a comparable minimalist approach to that in Wooster Street. Besides the sculptural ceiling (with a central element that conceals the ventilation duct), everything was taken out: plastered walls provide a neutral background and focus attention on two expressive shelves made of brushed steel elements and the cash register. The mirror is located at the back of the building, and one has to go through the whole shop to look at oneself in the mirror.

DISPLAY   In 1998, when asked to refurbish three shops with the same flair (Tokyo, Paris and New York), Future Systems and Kawasaki designed an abstract world, made out of objects that tend to blur one's sense of reality and balance. These are environments without scale, filled with island-like furniture, where clients forget reality and concentrate on clothes and accessories displayed in niches in the floor. It is a space like a museum, a retail version of the white cube so popular in art galleries.

After minimalism, after abstraction, Guerrilla shops are playing with another notion, that of invisibility. They recall older forms of retail, like remainder bookshops or clearance houses. They also take advantage of the existing situation and, with a minimum budget, demonstrate that anything can be used as display elements for Comme des Garçons's products. Here, there is no will to impress, but rather a wish to precisely erase any preconception about luxury. These existing tenements have the power to evoke another, not fashion-related type of environment and therefore to focus one's attention on Kawakubo's items solely. In order to achieve this, these are displayed in a naturalistic way, completely accessible to anybody who dares to enter.

Sources:

Frankel, S., 'Global Fashion: Sink the Flagship', *The Independent on Sunday*, 21 March 2004, Online. Available www.gradewinner.com/p/articles/mi_qn4159/is_200403/ai_n12752914 (accessed 4 April 2006)

Malfatti, P., 'Places of Fashion', *Abitare*, 398, September 2000: 212–7

Sudjic, D., *Rei Kawakubo and Comme des Garçons*, New York: Rizzoli, 1990

www.future-systems.com

www.guerrilla-store.com

www.infomat.com/community/whoswho/biography/reikawakubo.html

10 Corso Como
1991
Concept by Carla Sozzani and
Kris Ruhs
10 Corso Como, Milan, Italy
(DESIGNER/CLIENT) (LOCATION)
(COMMUNICATION) (SALES)

01 ground floor, interior:
the women's department

The first concept shop arrived on the scene in London in 1987, when Terence Conrad opened his Conrad Shop, offering a selection of artifacts related to fashion, industrial design, furniture and art under the same roof. This retail formula is not so much based on the product itself (even though quality remains a determinant), but on the atmosphere and lifestyle that such an accumulation projects. Success

DESIGNER/CLIENT   depends mostly on the owner's ability to offer a first-rate selection.

After a long career in the worlds of fashion (as a model, stylist and entrepreneur) and media (as a journalist, publisher and editor),

Carla Sozzani first opened the photography and design gallery that bears her name in 1990, completing it with a shop that sells art books and music. Other spaces soon followed: the '10 Corso Como' store one year later, a bar/restaurant in 1998 and a small Bed & Breakfast called '3 rooms' in 2003. Conceived with an initial investment of only $200,000, this ensemble has proved to be incredibly successful and now belongs to a selective group of shops (including Colette in Paris, Fred Segal in Los Angeles and Dover Street Market in London) that form a circuit known to cosmopolitan shoppers.

Remarkably, 10 Corso Como is situated on the outskirts of the city, in a district dominated by the nearby Porta Garibaldi railway station. It is organized around a classic Milanese courtyard, with an old, two-storey, 2500 m² garage building with a conservatory as its main element. While the shop occupies most of the ground floor area (1200 m²), the other functions are spread around the courtyard.

LOCATION The quiet, set-back environment prevents annoyance from traffic and brouhaha from the city, but it is also a strategic tool. The shop actually offers its clientele two seemingly contradictory things: on the one hand, the assurance of meeting a worldly crowd with similar codes and tastes, on the other, the possibility of interaction with genuine

02 the courtyard   **123 10 Corso Como, Milan (1991)**

Milanese 'in the know' about their city. It is an international hot spot
where you can also catch a glimpse of local happenings.

But the remoteness of the shop implies a different form of retail,
not aimed at impulse buying such as that in traditional shopping areas.
Because interested customers have to find their way to 10 Corso Como,
links with the media necessarily go beyond mere publicity. Sozzani's

COMMUNICATION previous experiences in both fashion and media are apparent in many
of 10 Corso Como's features. Her intention was to create a three-
dimensional fashion magazine where, 'when turning the pages, you
have something different, but with the feeling that you can buy
everything immediately'.[1] The ensemble, with its different
components, offers a collage of cultural, social and commercial entities
that are typical of glossy publications. The open design, the quantity
of products presented and the unusual way in which they are displayed
hold the customer's attention, keep him or her moving from one corner
to the next – again as a magazine layout would do visually.

Sozzani's choices are based on her own experience of the
market she is targeting, while her network (represented, for instance,
by her sister Franca Sozzani, editor-in-chief of *Vogue Italia*, or her
artist partner Kris Ruhs) provides her with the necessary back-up
and publicity.

The bazaar-like organization, displaying products of different
natures next to each other (furniture, fashion, culture, music, lifestyle),
shows a real understanding of how current retail functions.

On several levels, 10 Corso Como can be described as a boutique
– in the nineteenth-century sense – because it offers a series of services

SALES to its customers. The selection made by Sozzani precisely answers the
questions induced by the profusion of information and choice

1
Carla Sozzani interview with Tim
Blanks for Fashion File. Online.
Available www.fashionfile.com/
displayFeatures.html (accessed
4 March 2006)

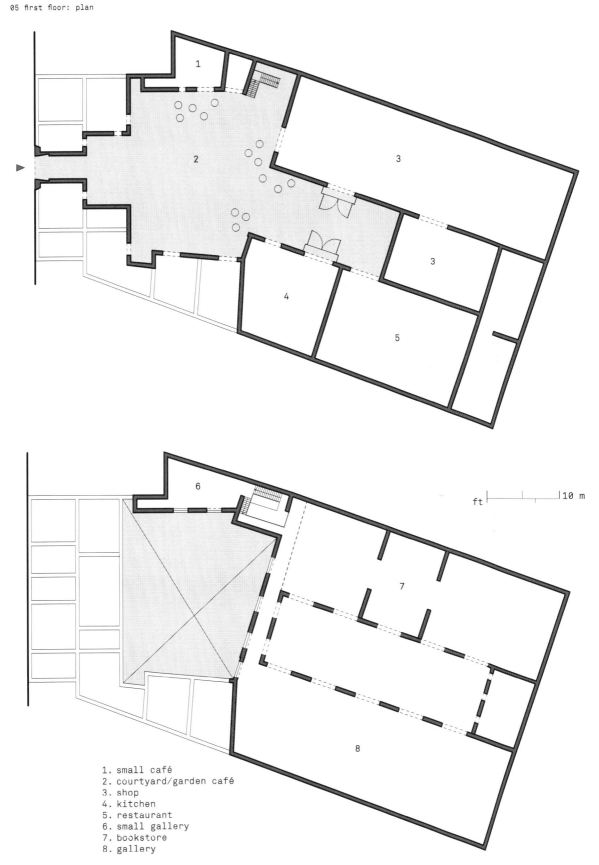

ft |————————|————————| 10 m

1. small café
2. courtyard/garden café
3. shop
4. kitchen
5. restaurant
6. small gallery
7. bookstore
8. gallery

06 first floor, interior:
the bookstore

presented by contemporary media. The central courtyard allows one to participate in a succession of socio-cultural activities: the gallery, the design store, the bookshop, the garden bar, the restaurant and the café. Significantly enough, the gallery came first and shopping is just one of many activities – all of which take advantage of their spatial proximity to each other. In this respect, 10 Corso Como not only gives access to new products, often hard-to-find imports, but most of all supports them by granting access to cultural references. It relocates them in design history and gives their potential owners the possibility to reconsider their own relation to design and art. The homey atmosphere of the place is fundamental, as it brings the customer closer to the

world evoked by the products, much more so than in a flagship store. As in a house, there is natural light, domestic furniture is used to display goods, there is a garden and a library, and even the possibility of having a drink; it is a place to stay (the B&B being the ultimate evidence of this), an aspect that might influence the sales volume.

Sources:

Horyn, C., 'The Talk: A Page Out of History', *New York Times*, 28 August 2005

www.galleriacarlasozzani.com

www.designboom.com/eng/funclub/10.html

Mandarina Duck
2000
NL Architects
219 rue St Honoré, Paris, France
(SALES) (COMMUNICATION) (DISPLAY)

01 ground floor: the cocoon

Italian leather goods company Mandarina Duck had to strategically reorganize its distribution network in the past ten years. This was partly due to the company's economic growth but also to the introduction of a clothing line that increased the number of items to be displayed in each shop.

The system developed to answer Mandarina Duck's new expectations was a retailing network including three types of shops.

SALES The 'embassies' are flagship stores located in fashionable European capitals like Milan, Berlin, Paris or London. With a sales area of about 300 m², they are designed by internationally renowned architects, giving each an autonomous character.

In cities like Florence or Lyons, the 'consulates' are medium-sized spaces (about 150 m²) with a standardized layout and fittings

02 ground floor: the pin wall
and the pallet tunnel

03 ground floor: the cocoon
and fluo-cupboards

(called 'Mandarina' and developed by Studio X Design Group) and a computerized stock and sales management system. Finally, 'corners' or 'focus areas' in selected department stores and multi-brand boutiques (designed according to the 'Mandarina' concept) ensure the presence of the brand and complete the network of globally recognizable retail points.

When asked to design the Parisian 'embassy', Dutch collective Droog Design approached NL Architects, who later went on to build the shop. The Dutch collective is known for its innovative designs that often reinterpret everyday artifacts, and has been a design culture favourite since its conception in 1993. The idea that Droog's founders **COMMUNICATION** Renny Ramakers and Gijs Bakker developed together with the architects was that of giving space the main role and of designing a

129 Mandarina Duck, Paris (2000)

store with no architecture, consisting only of furniture (including designs by Stijn Roodnat) and products.

This proved to be a very successful proposal on several levels: economically – the shop was a bestseller and its closure in February 2003 was only due to the brand's real estate strategy; as a marketing tool – because the shop was published in several prestigious magazines, Mandarina Duck realized that architecture could have an impact beyond its mere use; and as a trendsetter – some devices implemented in the shop were later reinterpreted and commercialized by other companies (fibreglass rods, colourful bike straps, etc.).

Even though only 40 per cent of the budget was used for furniture, its presence in the shop stands out, while the rest of the shop (around 130 m² ground floor and 190 m² first floor) was kept

DISPLAY neutral. Indeed, the original concept was to propose a set of various

05 first floor: the chain
curtain and the vacuum wall

06 ground floor: the pallet
tunnel and the entrance

objects that could be applied to any location and any future shop, and even though this idea was abandoned, it strongly defined the nature of these objects. They are autonomous elements (each of them reinterprets one aspect of retail), and together they cover the whole range of functions of a shop. For example, the revolving spiral staircase, a delicate piece of machinery next to the entrance, is meant

131 Mandarina Duck, Paris (2000)

Objects
1. revolving stair
2. pinwall
3. pallet tunnel
4. incubator
5. rubber wall
6. inverse clothing rack
7. counter
8. fitting rooms
9. vacuum wall
10. epoxy cupboard
11. stacked round tables
12. curtain room
13. socle
14. fluo-cupboards
15. mirrorboxes
16. grassland

Materials
1. painted steel
2. aluminium, id-polyethylene
3. lexaan excell, MDF
4. glass, MDF, steel
5. rhodorsil meélange-maitre MF 345 U
6. stainless steel
7. MDF, glass
8. mirror
9. UV stable PVC foil, steel
10. poured epoxy
11. steel
12. nickel-plated copper
13. lexaan excell, glass
14. metalmek armatures in steel frame
15. glass, MDF, steel
16. glass-fibre

132 Mandarina Duck, Paris (2000)

to catch the customer's eye and lead them to the second floor; the 'incubator' displays small and precious items that are normally protected behind glass in a playful way; on the 'pin wall', which resembles a child's toy, aluminium pipes can be pushed in or out of the surface. The 'inverse clothes rack' or 'cocoon' symbolizes the whole shop concept. Instead of displaying clothes, it hides them and provides an inner zone propitious to reasoned choices. It offers a good way to display a lot of items without making their presence too obvious.

The elements are free-standing, placed wherever they are necessary, and they all have a self-supporting lighting system. Their multiplicity makes it easy to replace one with another. The pallet tunnel, a back-lit object of translucent polycarbonate pallets specifically made for the shop, was later replaced by several showcases. These 'fluo-cupboards' are shelves made out of fluorescent light fixtures, in which products seem to be supported by light alone.

Besides displaying goods, some elements fulfil other functions: on the first floor, a heavy chain mail curtain acts as a space divider and fibreglass rods hide dressing rooms. The bright yellow cash desk at the back of the shop offers a view of the shop and has a long counter – to serve many customers and to display products and information.

Sources:

Colin, C., *Design et étalages*, Paris: Hazan, 2002, p. 174–5

Downey, C., 'Mandarina Duck', *Architectural Record*, 9, 2001

'Droog for Duck', *Domus*, 833, 2001: 52–63

Egg, A.L., 'Installation anti-conformiste', *Architecture intérieure créé*, 297, 2000: 70–1

Hunwick, P., 'An Open and Shut Case', *Blueprint*, December 2000: 50–2

Klauser, W., 'Winkel Mandarina Duck combineert perfecte organisatie met persoonlijke ondoordringbaarheid', *de Architect*, 32, 2001: 73–5

Nicolls, G., 'Duck à l'Orange', *Pi, project and interieur*, 2003

Nolan, B.,'Going Modular', *Frame*, 35, 2003: 42

www.mandarinaduck.com

Oki-ni
2001
6a architects
25 Savile Row, London, UK
(SALES) (LOCATION) (DISPLAY)

01 façade

The Oki-ni shop does not sell merchandise, it is a place where customers can discover and try on limited-edition clothes and accessories that they can then buy online. So it is not a boutique, but a physical extension of an e-shop. It also represents a new economic system, in which the lifespan of fashion goods is decreasing and where information and surprise are determinant characteristics. Oki-ni **SALES** consumers understand and accept these givens and in return the shop responds to this by providing them with a place connected to their (possibly idealized) way of living. A strong reference is the art gallery, with a shop where elements form an ephemeral installation rather than a definite selling space as the result. Some conventional retail elements have undergone a transformation: an informal information point has replaced the cash area, and storage, being superfluous here, has been reduced to a minimum. The space is wholly dedicated to displaying fashion items and gathering information.

LOCATION   However, the choice of location is both contrary to and the perfect counterpart of the interior design. Oki-ni has chosen to settle

02 detail: wall and hanging system

03 interior, general view

in Savile Row, London's tailors' street since the 1800s. By doing so, a parallel is created between tailor-making boutiques and the activities in this shop, with the idea that limited-edition items are nowadays custom-made suits. And keeping in mind the market Oki-ni is addressing: high-income customers who buy both high fashion and tailor-made clothes. Thus the location has a double function: it places Oki-ni into the segment it wants to be in, and provides customers with the confirmation of their own status. Smaller concessions can also be found in department stores in the UK. and Japan.

Display being the essence of this shop, the whole space can be defined as a showcase. Thanks to their detailing (simple window frames, painted black to reinforce the framing effect), the three large shop windows have minimal presence. The oak floor hovers above the existing structure, sloping up (in a 1:25 ratio) towards the back of the shop and wrapping up the walls. This technique, often used in stage design, visually increases the display area towards the street. The leftover spaces between this new skin and the irregular existing building envelope have been turned into changing rooms and storage areas.

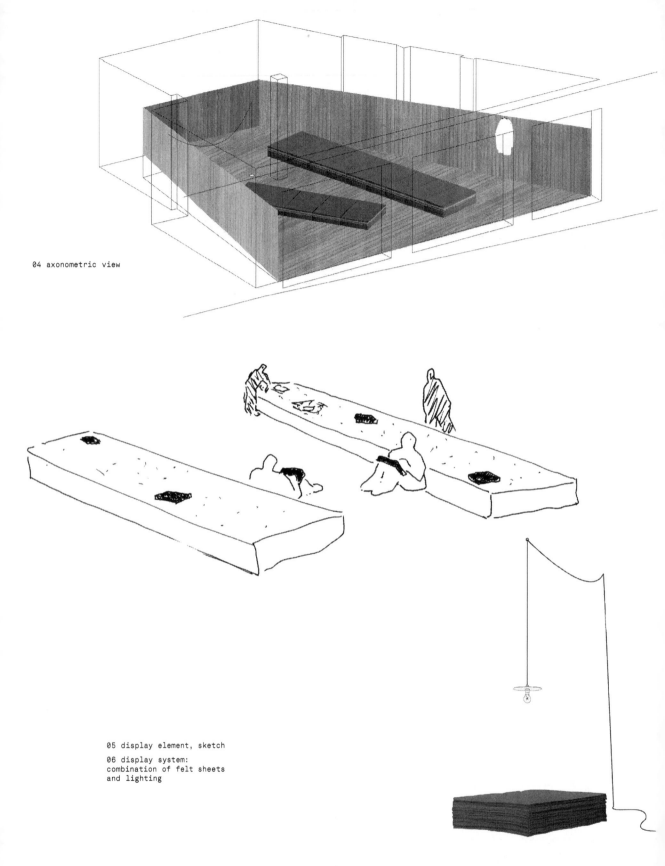

04 axonometric view

05 display element, sketch

06 display system:
combination of felt sheets
and lighting

136 Oki-ni, London (2001)

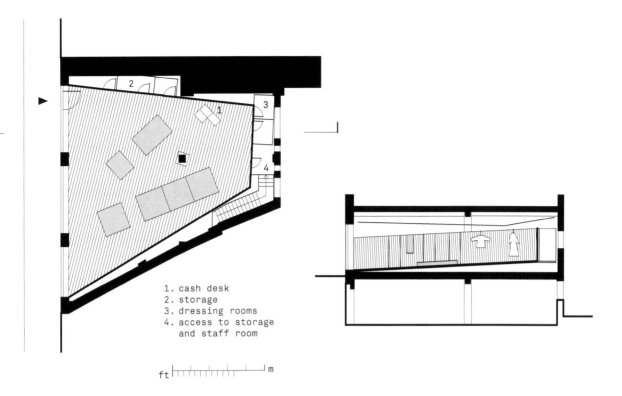

1. cash desk
2. storage
3. dressing rooms
4. access to storage
   and staff room

ft |⊢⊢⊢⊢⊢⊢⊢⊢⊢⊢⊢⊢—————⌐ m

07 plan
08 section

DISPLAY

On the wooden platform, piles of man-sized felt sheets serve as display elements with clothes lying on them. A single lamp hanging from the ceiling provides direct soft lighting to each pile (light being absorbed and evenly diffused by felt). These piles invite a loose way of shopping – customers can sit wherever they please, take time to check products, read magazines or order online from laptops. Coloured metal boxes complete the display possibilities. This system is multifunctional: felt sheets can be piled up into towers or spread across the floor, according to specific display requirements. Simple wire coat hangers dangle on the wooden walls.

There is an obviously designed informality to this shop, which is implemented by the softness and low-tech expression of all materials and finishing. Fluorescent neon lights give the space its general lighting, according to a grid that is directed towards the entrance, as a welcoming signal for potential customers.

Source:

www.oki-ni.com

137 Oki-ni, London (2001)

Camper Temporary Shop
'Walk in Progress'
2000
Marti Guixé
Various locations
(DESIGNER/CLIENT) (SALES) (MATERIALS)

01 interior, general view

Camper is a Spanish shoemaker, known for traditional, casual, yet innovative products, served by a strong ecological brand image. Marti Guixé has collaborated with Camper on several projects, first, as an industrial designer for merchandising items, then, from 1998 on, as the architect of Camper commercial spaces. He has worked on two specific projects: 'Walk in Progress', developed in 2000 for contemporary Camper shops waiting for definite interiors, and 'Best-Seller Shops', started in 2001 and aimed at highly functional shops. The first Walk in Progress shop was tested in Via Montenapoleone in Milan, and so far, six such Camper stores have been inaugurated.

The success of such a formula is due to Guixé's capacity to formulate simple rules that cover the whole range of archetypal components of a shop: façades, walls, lighting, displays. He chose to expose them on instruction cards like those for air crash procedures, a medium that is synthetic and can be understood by any shopkeeper.

Guixé's concept successfully addresses several constraints. First of all, it is more a set of rules than a definite model, a standard that can adapt to various situations. The idea is simple: to make a temporary and interactive shop that can be opened quickly and function efficiently until the final design is ready.

02 detail of the wall

These shop interiors also serve to express the brand image of nature, openness and awareness: they are built out of easily available, recyclable materials and clearly advertise this. By using shoeboxes as building bricks, the brand is present in the interior: discreetly, fleetingly, but nevertheless clearly.

They also give a central role to communication with the customer; they lend large participation to the retailer. These interiors manage to express a specific Camper philosophy and thus to provide environments that appeal to their target group. Communication is a recurrent theme in Camper's shops (for instance, the 'Info Shops' in 1998, in Barcelona, New York and London). By allowing customers to sign the walls (markers are handed out inside the store), they are given a role to play in an ephemeral art happening, making them part of Camper history. The performance is part of the shopping action.

But most of all, this formula gives Camper the possibility to answer the continuous business pressure that the company has been under because of its enormous success. Guixé manages to meet financial and time requirements: because most of their shops are located in prominent areas, Camper cannot afford to keep them closed while refurbishing. From nine to twelve months after the opening of a Walk in Progress shop, the permanent shop is opened.

To achieve this goal with the least amount of investment implies constructive and fitting systems that do not need specific skills or materials – systems that can be adapted to given situations while reusing, when possible, existing elements such as shop windows and lighting fittings.

Our architects and builders are now working on a unique project for reforming this space. We want to do the best job possible, which will take us at least nine to twelve months. Since we are a small company, we cannot afford to be closed for such a long time. We also think that having a store closed in an area as interesting as this is unfair to our colleagues. Meanwhile, we have opened this WALK IN PROGRESS STORE. We hope that you understand that, although the shoeboxes are not especially luxurious, the idea is simple, useful, and recyclable. The shoes are 100% CAMPER.

(Text on wall, explaining the renovation process)

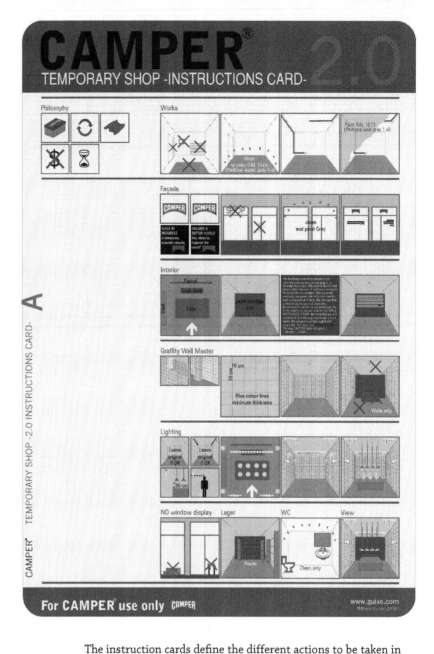

The instruction cards define the different actions to be taken in the shop interiors, according to the situation: how to clear the space; what colours to use on the walls, ceiling and floor; information to be applied to the façade; and the positions of display elements, pay desk and storage. The centre of the shop is decorated with a table made of **MATERIALS** shoeboxes on which the season's models are displayed. Walls are plastered white and a black grid defines squares in which customers are invited to write down their thoughts, messages or ideas. The only materials needed are paint and MDF for the shoeboxes. This simplicity and ease of execution also allow any shopkeeper to coordinate the renovation, whatever technical knowledge he/she may have. It is an economical, marketing and technical tool all in one.

140 Camper Temporary Shop, various locations (2000)

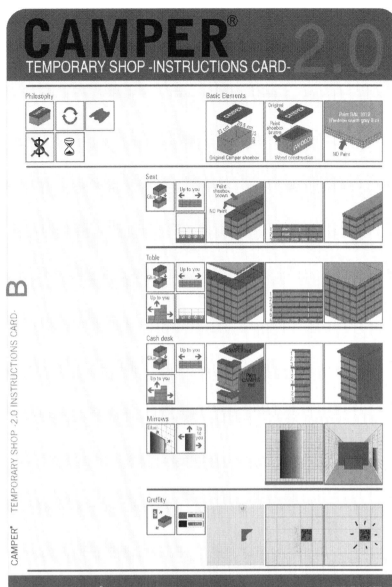

Sources:

Guixé, M., *1:1*, Rotterdam: 010 Publishers, 2002

Guixé, M., *Libre De Contexte / Context-Free / Kontext-Frei*, Basel: Birkhauser Verlag AG, 2004

www.camper.es

Camper Corporate Information, Online. Available www.camper.es/web/en/pdf/camper_corporate_info_en.pdf (accessed 12 March 2006)

www.guixe.com

141 Camper Temporary Shop, various locations (2000)

Australian Homemade Ice Cream
2002
Concrete Architectural Associates
Singel 437, Amsterdam,
The Netherlands
(DESIGNER/CLIENT) (LOCATION)
(SOCIAL ISSUES) (DISPLAY)

01 interior, general view

Originally a Belgian chain, ice cream-maker Australian Homemade developed a new image when introduced into the Netherlands in 1995. The success of the company lies in the quality of its products, all made using natural ingredients and flavours, but also in the implementation of new techniques. Thanks to their innovative production and stock management, Australian ice creams ingredients can be quickly transported; they are always fresh in the shop and can be transformed *ad hoc* without any specific know-how.

DESIGNER/CLIENT
Because they were not satisfied with the way their first shops looked, Australian's owners asked Concrete Architectural Associates to come up with a design that would provide a strong corporate identity. The result is a clear-cut, high-tech interior for young affluent consumers, with the Aboriginal theme standing for tradition, nature and mythology. This shop was the first to meet the expectations of the company, and its components were used to form a catalogue that would eventually be applied to other retail points.

As ice creams and their derivatives are products that are typically bought on impulse, they usually sell best along commercial routes. Australian therefore tends to locate its shops in specific locations, such as pedestrian areas, passages or shopping malls.

LOCATION
This first Dutch shop could be described as Australian's urban archetype: located in the heart of Amsterdam, on a corner where an important shopping street meets with a square, next to a flower market frequented by tourists. Although it is an indoor space, the presence of

02 detail of the counter
03 detail of the
refrigerators

143 Australian Homemade Ice Cream, Amsterdam (2002)

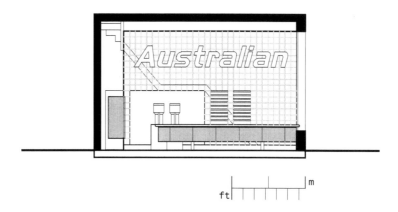

1. counter
2. access to storage and staff room
3. ice-cream machine

very large windows (a traditional aspect of Dutch ground-level architecture) maximizes the interaction between outside and inside. Thanks to its prominent location, with potential customers arriving from three different directions, consumption itself can be externalized: the nearby square with its benches and view of the canals and the market is a great place to sit and eat your ice cream.

Australian subtly plays with historical connotations, with components of the shop reminiscent of Italian *gelaterias*, an urban type going back to the nineteenth century. But while *gelaterias* are traditionally private-owned businesses, whose success is generally **SOCIAL ISSUES** based on personal craftsmanship, Australian chooses to advertise its particular production techniques. Instead of selling a specific

144 Australian Homemade Ice Cream, Amsterdam (2002)

know-how, it takes advantage of the latest developments to ensure constant quality.

Yet these two forms of retail, while rather different, are successfully brought together in the interior. The display counter has ice-cream containers with simple, wrought lids; everything is made on site from fresh, all-natural ingredients, with the help of turbines strategically left in sight; ice creams are not kept frozen, but close to room temperature in order to get the real taste. Australian pursues the traditional combination of offering coffee next to ice creams, but has enriched this to accommodate contemporary demands: beverages like hot chocolate, milkshakes or cold drinks, and chocolate bonbons.

The simplicity of the design responds to the simplicity of the concept. There is an attempt to display authenticity, through a combination of two components, each having a defined function. The 'Australian' flair is to be found everywhere, from the use of aboriginal patterns on packaging, chocolate finishing and flooring, to the use of sandy colours. It transmits the brand and ensures that the **DISPLAY** shop stays agreeable and appealing to a large crowd. On the other hand, the specific conditioning constraints of this type of product have been addressed radically and literally: all display elements (the counter for ice-cream containers and chocolate bonbons; seven fridges in the back wall for chocolate packs and drinks) are made out of stainless steel, expressing a hygienic connotation inherent to food products. The fridges, by their shape, size and commonness, resemble those in supermarkets. They are immediately recognizable to the customer and therefore directly usable.

Lighting plays an important role in that it regulates the overall atmosphere of the shop. Fittings subtly diffuse warm (yellow) lighting during winter months and cold lighting (whiter) during the summer. This system allows the company to regulate the background against which transactions are made, and to influence them. Here, the cooperation between merchandising and architecture works perfectly. By evoking the background of a *gelateria* and by sharing simple decorative elements with merchandising, this design offers a highly recognizable archetype in a time of mass production.

Sources:

www.australianhomemade.com

www.australianicecream.be

Duchi shoe shop
2004
2012 Architecten
Palaceplein 252, Scheveningen,
the Netherlands
(DESIGNER/CLIENT)
(MATERIALS) (DISPLAY)

01 interior, general view

The theme of recycling is central to 2012 Architecten's work. This group of young architects based in Rotterdam tries to produce viable architecture from waste, along with developing a digital catalogue (www.recyclicity.net) and encouraging designers to reuse the materials listed there, which are cheap and often available in huge quantities.

DESIGNER/CLIENT 2012 Architecten develop their ideas through their projects, both theoretical and real. The Duchi shoe shop, located in The Hague seaside resort of Scheveningen, gave 2012 Architecten a chance to explore and put into practice their principles. However, one cannot help noticing that the products sold here (a large range of shoes for young-minded people) do not necessarily adhere to the ecological statement the shop seems to wish to identify with. The use of recycled material is not evident in the product; the ecological preoccupation it presupposes is solely used as a way to appeal to a crowd – possibly politically conscious, certainly sensitive to uncommon designs.

02 the wooden bench as fitting element
below
03 detail of the shelves

MATERIALS

The recycled materials used here evoke specific worlds (the car and building industries); the designers sublimated these and managed to redirect them into the service of the newly created environment and the realm unconsciously linked to this type of products.

Some 90 per cent of the fittings in the 70 m² shop are composed of waste, and the use of discarded materials or leftovers had consequences on several levels. The specifics of these materials (in terms of shape, building qualities and amount of reworking their original rough state demanded) have been taken into account. Obliged to adapt to existing dimensions and time-consuming treatment, the architects did not to try to fit the existing premises. Instead, they concentrated on finding simple and striking elements that were both representative and multifunctional (luckily enough, the circular shelf units fit perfectly into the existing dimensions). For this reason, and except for the central sitting furniture, no element was conceived before actually being placed in the shop; the design took place during the building process.

The space along the shop front is kept free for displaying and paying; further back, two main elements give the interior space its organization: a central 'trying-out element' and a circular, continuous storage shelf around it. The existing premises (walls and ceilings) and a small enclosed space (containing the locker and toilets) have been kept neutral and are used as a backdrop for the design.

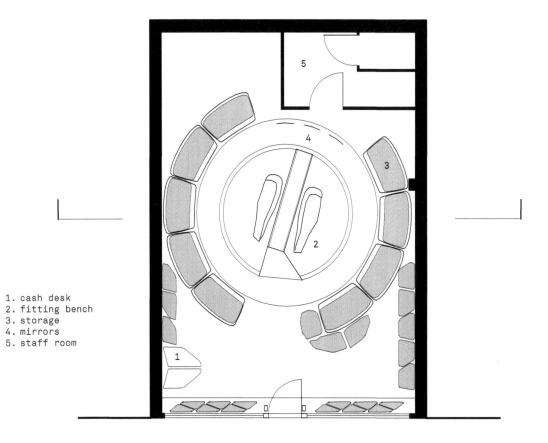

1. cash desk
2. fitting bench
3. storage
4. mirrors
5. staff room

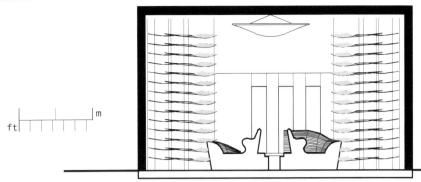

ft |_____| m

With a diameter of 4 m and a complex organic shape, the central island serves multiple functions: it offers seats and backrests for the clients and is also a footstool at working height for the salespeople. Customers can try out footwear in its centre by walking on an old cash register conveyer belt. The entire floor of the shop, covered with recycled wood, has been raised in order to hide its machinery.

The surface of this piece of furniture is made of about 1500 off-cuts from various wood types (40 x 2 cm, in pine, birch, acacia and mahogany), glued and hooked onto a plywood construction, then

DISPLAY sanded and finished.

The storage shelves surrounding the sitting element are made of Audi 100 windscreens. For the shop window and the cash-desk case, thirty more frontal and forty lateral windscreens were used. These windscreens are no longer in production, but their discovery in a depot formed the starting point for the design. They are arranged parallel to one another and form a circular shelf that is used to store and display the different products of all sizes. This arrangement offers both personnel and clientele a better screening of available products: it eases work and at the same time tempts customers to check out other products that would normally be hidden in a separate stock room.

Besides their ecological dimension, these two elements also correspond to some specific social interactions: they permit a fluid, effortless exchange between customers and personnel, soften the spatial division and turn the shop into a convenient place to be in. The windscreens are fixed on a stainless-steel structure that represents the only brand new element. Recycling was not possible here, because of the specific shape of the shelves, but also because of the harsh salty North Sea climate that demands specifically resistant material.

Sources:

Erven, R., 'Ontwerpen met afvalstromen', *de Architect*, October 2004

Uhde, R., *Aus zweiter Hand*, Online, 2004. Available www.robert-uhde.de/html/referenz_dyn.php (accessed 13 January 2006)

www.2012architecten.nl

www.recyclicity.net

149 Duchi, Scheveningen (2004)

While this book discusses retail architecture through the model of the boutique, the argument cannot be reduced to one type. The aim of this bibliography is to provide the reader with a tool for further reading.

The bibliography has been divided in two parts: the first presents books and articles on consumer culture, retail and economy history. The second concentrates on architecture, with links to other typologies or specific points of interests such as shop fronts.

Consumer culture and economic history

General

Alexander, D., *Retailing in England during the Industrial Revolution*, London: Athlone Press, 1970

Alexander, N. and Akehurst, G. (eds), *The Emergence of Modern Retailing, 1750–1950*, London: Frank Cass Publishers, 1998

Appadurai, A. (ed.), *The Social Life of Things: Commodities in Cultural Perspective*, Cambridge: Cambridge University Press, 1988

Baren, M., *Victorian Shopping*, London: Trafalgar Square, 1999

Bataille, G., *The Accursed Share: An Essay on General Economy, vol. 1: Consumption*, trans. R. Hurley, New York: Zone Books, 1991

Baudrillard, J., *The Consumer Society: Myths and Structures*, London: Sage, 1998

Bayley, S. (ed.), *Commerce and Culture*, London: Penshurst Press, 1989

Benson, J., *The Rise of Consumer Society in Britain, 1880–1980*, London: Longman, 1994

Benson, J. and Shaw, G. (eds), *The Evolution of Retail Systems, c.1800–1914*, Leicester: Leicester University Press, 1992

Benson, J. and Ugolini, L. (eds), *A Nation of Shopkeepers: Five Centuries of British Retailing*, London: I.B. Tauris and Co., 2003

Berg, M. and Clifford, H. (eds), *Consumers and Luxury: Consumer Culture in Europe 1650–1850*, Manchester: Manchester University Press, 1999

Bluestone, B., Hanna, P., Kuhn, S. and Moore, L., *The Retail Revolution: Market Transformation, Investment and Labor in the Modern Department Store*, Boston: Auburn House Publishing Company, 1981

Bowlby, R., *Just Looking: Consumer Culture in Dreiser, Gissing and Zola*, London: Methuen, 1985

Bowlby R., *Carried Away: The Invention of Modern Shopping*, New York: Columbia University Press, 2001

Braudel, F., *Civilization and Capitalism, 15th–18th Century, vol. 2: Wheels of Commerce*, trans. S. Reynolds, Berkeley, CA: University of California Press, 1992. Civilisation matérielle, économie et capitalisme, XVe–XVIIIe siècle. Les jeux de l'échange, vol. 2, Paris: LGF-Livre de Poche, 1993

Brewer, J. and Porter, R., *Consumption and the World of Goods*, London: Routledge, 1993

Britnell, R., *The Commercialisation of English Society 1000–1500*,
    Cambridge: Cambridge University Press, 1994

Carrier, J. G., *Gifts and Commodities: Exchange and Western
    Capitalism since 1700*, London: Routledge, 1995

Chung C. J., Inaba, J., Koolhaas, R. and Leong, S. T., *The Harvard Design
    School Guide to Shopping: Harvard Design School Project on the City 2*,
    Köln: Taschen, 2001

Corrigan, P., *The Sociology of Consumption: An Introduction*, London: Sage
    Publications, 1997

Cowen, T., *In Praise of Commercial Culture*, Cambridge, MA: Harvard
    University Press, 1998

Cox, N., *The Complete Tradesman: A Study of Retailing, 1550–1820*,
    Burlington, VT: Ashgate, 2000

Cummings, N. and Lewandowska, M., *The Value of Things*, Basel:
    Birkhäuser, 2000

Dannhaeuser, N., *Concentration of Trade and Its Urban Impact Under
    Capitalism and Socialism: Former West Germany (Hassfurt) and East
    Germany (Hildburghausen) Compared*, London: Routledge, 1994

Davis, D., *A History of Shopping*, London: Routledge & Kegan Paul, 1966

Deane, P., *The First Industrial Revolution*, Cambridge: Cambridge
    University Press, 1965

Douglas, M. and Isherwood, B., *The World of Goods: Towards an
    Anthropology of Consumption*, New York: Basic Books, 1979

Epstein, S., *Wage and Labor Guilds in Medieval Europe*, Chapel Hill, NC:
    University of North Carolina Press, 1991

Evans, B. and Lawson, A., *A Nation of Shopkeepers*, London: Plexus,
    1981

Farrell, J., *One Nation under Goods: Malls and the Seduction of American
    Shopping*, Washington, DC: Smithsonian Institute Press, 2003

Fine, B. and Leopold, E., *The World of Consumption: The Material and
    Cultural Revisited, 2nd edn*, London: Routledge, 2002

Fogg, M., *Boutique: A 60s Cultural Phenomenon*, London: Mitchell
    Beazley, 2003

Fraser, W. H., *The Coming of the Mass Market, 1850–1914*, Hamdon, CT:
    Archon Books, 1981
    The book analyses the relationship between the emergence of
    mass production, retailing and marketing in the UK. The author
    discusses mostly small shops, so there is very little on the
    influence of the department store in fostering a mass
    market/mass consumption society.

Gadd, I. A. and Wallis, P. (eds), *Guilds, Society, and Economy in London,
    1450–1800*, London: Centre for Metropolitan History, Institute of
    Historical Research, 2002

Gardner, C. and Sheppard, J., *Consuming Passion: The Rise of Retail
    Culture*, London: HarperCollins Publishers, 1989

Gottdiener, M., *New Forms of Consumption: Consumers, Culture, and
    Commodification*, New York: Barnes & Noble, 2000

Harrison, M., *People and Shopping: A Social Background*, Totowa, NJ: Rowman and Littlefield, 1975

Havenhand, G., *A Nation of Shopkeepers*, London: Eyre and Spottiswoode, 1970

Jefferys, J. B., *Retail Trading in Britain, 1850–1950*, Cambridge: Cambridge University Press, 1954

This book traces British retailing not only in general but by trade area as well (i.e. grocery, meat, milk, clothing, footwear, furniture, etc.). Jefferys makes a clear distinction between the retail trade before 1914, from 1914 to 1939, and 1939 to 1950, with three separate chapters analysing the distributive trades of each period. A fourth chapter looks at the development of large-scale retailing.

Jeremy, D., *A Business History of Britain, 1900–1990s*, Oxford: Oxford University Press, 1998

This book proposes a synthesis on the evolution of marketing and marketing methods in the twentieth century.

Jones, K. and Simmons, J., *The Retail Environment*, London: Routledge, 1990

Kellett, J. W., 'The Breakdown of Guild and Corporation Control over the Handicraft and Retail Trades of London', *Economic History Review*, 10930, April 1958: 381–94

Larkin, J., *The Reshaping of Everyday Life, 1790–1840*, New York: Harper & Row, 1988

MacKendrick, N., Brewer, J. and Plumb, J. H. (eds), *The Birth of Consumer Society: The Commercialization of Eighteenth Century England*. Bloomington, IN: Indiana University Press, 1982

Miami University, *History of Economics*, Online. Available http://eh.net/HE (accessed 13 February 2006)

This website provides resources and promotes communication among scholars in economic history and related fields. Bibliography, book reviews and encyclopedia.

Miller, D., *Material Culture and Mass Consumption*, Oxford: Blackwell, 1987

Miller, D. (ed.), *Shopping, Place, and Identity*, New York: Routledge, 1998

Miller, D., *The Dialectics of Shopping (1998 Morgan Lectures)*, Chicago: University of Chicago Press, 2001

Pegler, M. M., *Retail Entertainment*, New York: Watson-Guptill Publications, 1998

Peterson, R. A., *The Future of U.S. Retailing: An Agenda for the 21st Century*, Westport, CT: Quorum Books, 1992

Randall, A. E., 'The "Perestroika" of Soviet Retail Trade: Visionary Planning for a Revolution in Retailing', unpublished thesis, University of Mississippi, 2004

Richardson, G., *Medieval Guilds*, Online. Available http://eh.net/encyclopedia/article/richardson.guilds (accessed 13 February 2006)

Salzmann, L. F., *English Trade in the Middle Ages*, Oxford, 1931

Schlereth, T. J., *Victorian America: Transformations in Everyday Life,
1876–1915*, New York: HarperCollins, 1991

Seid, M. H., *Where It All Began: The Evolution of Franchising*, Online.
Available www.msaworldwide.com/upload/History%20
of%20Franchising.pdf (accessed 4 January 2006)

Shaw, G., Curth. L. and Alexander, A., *Selling Self-Service and the
Supermarket: The Americanisation of Food Retailing in Britain,
1945–60*, London: Routledge, 2004

Slater, D., *Consumer Culture and Modernity*, Cambridge: Polity Press,
1997

Slater, D., *Consumer Culture Bibliography*, Online. Available
http://homepages.gold.ac.uk/slater/consumer/biblioa.htm
(accessed 4 May 2006)
Very complete bibliography on consumer culture literature.

Stearns, P. N., *Consumerism in World History: The Global Transformation
of Desire*, New York: Routledge, 2002

Strasser, S., McGovern, C. *et al.* (eds), *Getting and Spending: European
and American Consumer Societies in the Twentieth Century*,
Cambridge: Cambridge University Press, 1998

Watson, J., *Literature and Material Culture from Balzac to Proust: The
Collection and Consumption of Curiosities*, Cambridge: Cambridge
University Press, 1999

Williams, R., *Dream Worlds: Mass Consumption in Late Nineteenth-
Century France*, Berkeley, CA: University of California
Press, 1982

Contemporary criticism

Augé, M., *Non-Places: Introduction to an Anthropology of Supermodernity*,
London and New York: Verso, 1995

Bryman, A., *Disneyization of Society*, Thousand Oaks, CA: Sage, 2004

Debord, G., *The Society of the Spectacle*, trans. D. Nicholson-Smith,
New York: Zone Books, 1995

Forty, A., *Objects of Desire: Design and Society, 1750–1980*, London:
Thames and Hudson, 1986

Klein, N., *No Logo: Taking Aim at the Brand Bullies*, Toronto: Vintage,
2000

Ritzer, G., *The McDonaldization of Society*, London: Pine Forge Press,
2004.

Sorkin, M. (ed.), *Variations on a Theme Park: The New American City
and the End of Public Space*, New York: Hill and Wang, 1992

Zukin, S., Point of Purchase: *The Transformation of Shopping into
Public Culture*, London: Routledge, 2003
This book addresses the influence of shopping on post-war
American society.

Gender

Shopping played an important role in social and cultural sexual differentiation, and several books have investigated this aspect of retail in terms of architecture, social changes and economy.

Abelson, E. S., *When Ladies Go A-Thieving: Middle Class Shoplifters in the Victorian Department Store*, New York: Oxford University Press, 1989

Adburgham, A., *Shops and Shopping, 1800–1914: Where, and in What Manner the Well-Dressed Englishwoman Bought her Clothes*, London: Allen and Unwin, 1964

Benson, S. P., *Counter Culture: Saleswomen, Managers and Customers in American Department Stores, 1890–1940*, Urbana, IL: University of Illinois Press, 1988

Cook, D., *Maleshop: Men, Consumerism and Shopping*, New York: Lawrence & Wishart, 1995

Kowaleski-Wallace, E., *Consuming Subjects: Women, Shopping, and Business in the Eighteenth Century*, New York: Columbia University Press, 1997

Mort, F., *Cultures of Consumption: Masculinities and Social Space in Late Twentieth-Century Britain*, London and New York: Routledge, 1996

Nava, M., *Changing Cultures: Feminism, Youth and Consumerism*, London: Sage, 1992

Rappaport, E., '"The Halls of Temptation": Gender, Politics, and the Construction of the Department Store in Victorian London', *Journal of British Studies*, 35, January 1996

The architecture of commerce

General

Artley, A., *The Golden Age of Shop Design: European Shop Interiors, 1880–1939*, London: Architectural Press, 1975

Barreneche, R., *New Retail*, London: Phaidon Press, 2005

Blaisse, L. and Gaillard, F., *Temps Denses 1*, Paris: Editions de l'Imprimeur, 1999; *Temps Denses 2*, Paris: Teraedre, 2003
Two comparative essays on contemporary design in five different fields: fashion, health, architecture, advertisement and industrial design.

Colin, C. (ed.), *Design et étalages*, Paris: Industries françaises de l'Ameublement/Seuil, 2002

Din, R., *New Retail*, London: Conran Octopus, 2000

Hocquel, W., Kellermann, F., Pfeifer, H.-G., Schreiber, M., Weiss, K.-D. and Zeidler, E. H., *Architecture for the Retail Trade: Department Stores, Shopping Centres, Arcades, History and Current Tendencies*, Basel: Birkhäuser, 1996

Jarry, P., *Les magasins de nouveautés: histoire rétrospective et anecdotique*, Paris: André Barry et fils, 1948

Lefuel, H., *Boutiques parisiennes du Premier Empire*, Paris, 1926

Lehbar, G. M., *Chain Stores in America 1859–1962*, New York: Chain Store Publishing Corp., 1963

Mayo, J. M., *The American Grocery Store: The Business Evolution of an Architectural Space*, Westport, CT: Greenwood Press, 1993

Morrison, K. A., *English Shops and Shopping: An Architectural History*, New Haven, CT: Yale University Press, 2003

Pevsner, N., *A History of Building Types*, Princeton, NJ: Princeton University Press, 1976

Riewoldt, O., *Retail Design*, Amsterdam: BIS Publishers, 2000

Riewoldt, O., *Brandscaping: Worlds of Experience in Retail Design*, Basel: Birkhäuser, 2002

Ruston, P., *Out of Town Shopping: The Future of Retailing*, London: British Library, 1999

Schuhmacher, A., *Ladenbau*, Stuttgart: Julius Hoffmann, 1934
This comprehensive book on shops offers around 75 plates of details of construction of shops, and photographs of many examples in both Europe and America.

On market places

Bailly, G-H. and Laurent, P., *La France des halles et marchés*, Toulouse: Privat, 1998

Baltard, V. and Callet, F., *Monographie des Halles Centrales de Paris*, Paris: Ducher, 1872
This is probably the best record of Les Halles, the central market hall in Paris that was destroyed in 1971. The introduction is historical and technical and the plates range from a sweeping bird's-eye view to the smallest detail.

Brown, J., *The English Market Town: A Social and Economic History, 1750–1914*, Ramsbury: Crowood Press, 1986

Chartres, J. A., *Internal Trade in England, 1500–1700*, London: Macmillan, 1977

De Voe, T. F., *The Market Book: A History of the Public Markets of the City of New York*, 1862, reprinted New York: Augustus M. Kelley, 1970

Hilton, R. H., 'Medieval Market Towns and Simple Commodity Production', *Past and Present*, 109, November, 1985: 3–23

Letters, S., *Online Gazetteer of Markets and Fairs in England and Wales to 1516*, Online. Available www.history.ac.uk/cmh/gaz/gazweb2.html (accessed 13 April 2006)
The Gazeteer's website proposes its own bibliography on British medieval marketplaces. This is regularly updated and goes through a range of sources to provide as much information as possible about each market.

On arcades

Benjamin, W., *The Arcades Project*, trans. H. Eiland and K. McLaughlin, Cambridge, MA: Belknap Press, 1999

Carughi, U., *La Galleria Umberto I: architettura del ferro a Napoli*,
    Napoli: F. Di Mauro

Delorme, J.-C. and Dubois, A.-M., *Passages couverts parisiens*, Paris:
    Parigramme, 1996

De Moncan, P., *Les passages en Europe*, Paris: Editions du mécène, 1993

Geist, J. F., *Arcades: History of a Building Type*, London: MIT Press, 1982

Lemoine, B., *Les Passages couverts en France*, Paris: Délégation à l'Action
    artistique de la Ville de Paris, 1989

MacKeith, M., *The History and Conservation of Shopping Arcades*,
    London: Mansell, 1986

White, A. G., *Architecture of Arcades and Galleria: A Selected Bibliography*,
    Monticello, IL: Vance Bibliographies, 1984

On department stores

Bragg, A., 'Will the Department Store Survive?', *Sales and Marketing
    Management*, 136, April 1986

Cohen, D., 'Grand Emporiums Peddle Their Wares in a New Market',
    Smithsonian, 23(12), March 1993

Parker, K. W., 'Sign Consumption in the 19th-Century Department
    Store: An Examination of Visual Merchandising in the Grand
    Emporiums (1846–1900)', *Journal of Sociology*, 39, 2003

Schoenherr, S. E., *Evolution of the Department Store, 2004*. Online.
    Available http://history.sandiego.edu/gen/soc/shopping
    center4.html (accessed 27 December 2005)
    The website provides a bibliography.

Tamilia, R.D., *The Wonderful World of the Department Store in Historical
    Perspective: A Comprehensive International Bibliography Partially
    Annotated*, 2002. Online. Available http://faculty.quinnipiac.
    edu/charm/dept.store.pdf (accessed 27 December 2005)
    This survey of existing literature on department stores is very
    complete and forms an excellent departure point for anybody
    interested in the evolution of this specific typology, or on
    shopping in general.

On shopping malls

Balachandran, M., *Malls and Shopping Centers: A Selected Bibliography,
    1970–1975*, Monticello, IL: Council of Planning Librarians, 1976

Beddington, N., *Shopping Centres: Retail Development, Design, and
    Management*, London: Architectural Press, 1991

Borking, S., *Fascinating History of Shopping Malls*, The Hague: MAB
    Group, 1998

Brambilla, R., *American Urban Malls: A Compendium*, New York: Institute
    for Environmental Action, 1977

Casazza, J. A. and Spink, F. H., *Shopping Center Development Handbook*,
    Washington, DC: Urban Land Institute, 1992

Cohen, N. E., *America's Market Places: The History of Shopping Centers*,
    Lyme, CT: Greenwich, 2002

Cohen, Y. S., *Diffusion of an Innovation in an Urban System: The Spread of Planned Regional Shopping Centers in the United States, 1849–1968*, Chicago: Geography Department, University of Chicago, 1972

Dawson, J. A., *Shopping Centers: A Bibliography*, Chicago: CPL Bibliographies, 1982
This book offers a good bibliography up to the early 1980s for books in other European countries, including Germany, the Netherlands, Belgium, Italy and Spain.

Gruen, V., 'The Sad Story of Shopping Centers', *Town and Country Planning*, 46, 1978

Gruen, V. and Smith, L. P., 'Shopping Centers: The New Building Type', *Progressive Architecture*, 33, June 1952

Gruen, V. and Smith, L. P., *Shopping Towns USA: The Planning of Shopping Centers*, New York: Reinhold Pub. Corp., 1960
The three texts by Victor Gruen clearly show his changes of mind towards the typology he helped to invent.

Hardwick, M. J., *Victor Gruen: Mall Maker, Architect of an American Dream*, Philadelphia, PA: University of Pennsylvania Press, 2003

Kowinski, W., *The Malling of America: An Inside Look at the Great Consumer Paradise*. New York: William Morrow, 1985

Longstreth, R. W., *The Drive-In, the Supermarket, and the Transformation of Commercial Space in Los Angeles, 1914–1941*, Cambridge, MA: MIT Press, 1999

Maitland, B., *Shopping Malls: Planning and Design*, New York: Nichols, 1985

Muller, T., *Central Business Districts, Cities, and Shopping Malls*, Washington, DC: Urban Land Institute, 1978

Orr, J. F., *Malls, Pedestrian Malls, and Shopping Centers: A Selected Bibliography with Annotations*, Monticello, IL: Vance Bibliographies, 1979

Vance, M., *Bibliography on Shopping Centers*, Monticello, IL: Vance Bibliographies, 1982.

Vance, M., *Shopping Centers: Recent Journal Articles*, Monticello, IL: Vance Bibliographies, 1988

On other forms of retail

Berry, J. and Roberts, M., *Co-op Management and Employment*, London: ICOM Co-Publications, 1984

De Bernardi, J. M., *The Catalog Showroom Formula*, New York: Chain Store Age Books, 1974

Fitoussi, B., *Showrooms*, Princeton, NJ: Princeton Architectural Press, 1990

Medla, K., *Shop-in-the-shop: ein Konzept der Angebotspräsentation im Einzelhandel*, München: Florentz, 1987

Nightingale, J., *The Bazaar: Its Origin, Nature and Objects*, London, 1816

Pegler, M. M., *Market, Supermarket and Hypermarket Design*, New York: Van Nostrand Reinhold International, 1992

Technical handbooks

Barr, V., *Designing to Sell: A Complete Guide to Retail Store Planning and Design*, New York: McGraw-Hill, 1986
This guide has a complete chapter on lighting techniques.

Barr, V., *Building Type Basics for Retail and Mixed-Use Facilities*, New York: Wiley, 2004

Bellenger, D. and Goldstucker, J. I., *Retailing Basics*, Homewood, IL: RD Irwin, 1983

Buxton, A., *The Cash Railway Website*, Online. Available http://cashrailway.co.uk (accessed 10 January 2006)
Comprehensive bibliography on cash handling systems in shops and department stores from the 1880s to the present day.

Cliff, S., *50 Trade Secrets of Great Design Retail Spaces*, Gloucester, MA: Rockport Publishers, 1999

Gosling, D. and Maitland, B., *The Design and Planning of Retail Systems*, New York: Whitney Library of Design, 1976

Green, W., *The Retail Store: Design and Construction*, New York: Van Nostrand Reinhold, 1986

Hammond, A. E., *Store Interior Planning and Display*, London: Blandford, 1939

Hartnell, A. P., *Shop Planning and Design*, London: 1944

The Institute of Store Planners, *Stores and Retail Spaces* series, Cincinnati: St Media Group International, 2000

Israel, L. J., *Store Planning/Design*, Hoboken, NJ: Wiley, 1994

Ketchum, M., *Shops and Stores*, New York: Reinhold, 1957

Kiesler, F., *Contemporary Art Applied to the Store and Its Display*, New York: Brentano's Publishers, 1930

Kooijman, D., *Machine and Theatre: Design Concepts for Shop Buildings (Machine en theater: Ontwerpconcepten van winkelgebouwen)*, Rotterdam: 010 Publishers, 1999

Lamacraft, J., *Retail Design: New Store Experiences*, London: FT Retail and Consumer, 1998

Liffen, J., 'The Development of Cash Handling Systems for Shops and Department Stores', *Transactions of the Newcomen Society*, 71(1), 1999–2000: 79–101

Mun, D., *Shops: A Manual of Planning and Design*, London: Architectural Press, 1981

Nicholson, E., *Contemporary Shops in the United States*, New York: Architectural Book Publishing Company, 1945

Nystrom, P., *Retail Selling and Store Management*, New York: Appleton, 1925

Nystrom, P., *Economics of Retailing*, New York: Arno Press, 1978

Pain, G. M, *Planning and the Shopkeeper; with Particular Reference to the Problem of Commercial Deliveries to and from Shops*, London: Barrie and Rockliff, 1967

Parnes, L., *Planning Stores That Pay: Organic Design and Layout for Efficient Merchandising*, New York: F. W. Dodge Corporation, 1948

Snider, J., *Future Shop: How New Technologies Will Change the Way We Shop and What We Buy*, New York: St. Martin's Press, 1992

Somake, E. E., *Shops and Stores Today; Their Design, Planning and Organisation*, London: Batsford, 1956

Towsey, R. G., *Self Service Retailing*, London: ILIFFE Books, 1964

Trystan Edwards, A., *The Architecture of Shops*, London: Chapman & Hall., 1933
This book discusses the treatment of the shopping street, methods of display of merchandise, advertisements and signs. Illustrated with 84 diagrams and photographs.

Turner, J., *Retail Spaces: Lighting Solutions for Shops, Malls and Markets*, Crans-près-Céligny: RotoVision, 1998

Westwood, B. and Westwood, N., *The Modern Shop*, London: Architectural Press, 1952

On shop windows and display techniques

Chatterton, F., *Shop Fronts: A Selection of English, American and Continental Examples*, London: The Architectural Press, 1927
This book includes a number of traditional English examples.

Dan, H. and Wilmont, M., *English Shop Fronts, Old and New*, London: B. T. Batsford, 1907

Dean, D., *English Shopfronts: From Contemporary Source Books, 1792–1840*, London, 1970

English Heritage, *Shopfronts: Listed Building Guidance Leaflet*, London: English Heritage, 1990

Herbst, R., *Modern French Shop-Fronts and their Interiors*, London: J. Tiranti, 1927
48 photographs of shop fronts and interiors.

Portas, M., *Windows: The Art of Retail Display*, London: Thames & Hudson, 2001

Powers, A., *Shopfronts*, London: Chatto and Windus, 1989

Roth, L., *Display Design: An Introduction to Window Display, Point-of-Purchase, Posters, Signs and Signage, Sales Environments, and Exhibit Displays*, Englewood Cliffs, NJ: Prentice-Hall, 1983

Tucker, J., *Retail Desire: Design, Display and Visual Merchandising*, Crans-près-Céligny: RotoVision, 2005

Walsh, C., 'Shop Design and the Display of Goods in Eighteenth-Century London', *Journal of Design History*, 8, 1995

A
America 5, 6, 58, 62
Amsterdam 46, 142, 143
Asia 58, 59
Athens 114
Austria 71, 94

B
Barcelona 48, 52, 139
Berlin 73, 114, 119, 128
Britain 4, 5

C
Cologne 114
Corso Monforte 100

D
Dresden 66, 67, 108
    Bautzner Strasse 66

E
England 41
Europe 8, 24, 38, 41, 58, 59, 86
    Middle East 58
    Northern Europe 28, 47
    Western Europe 3

F
Florence 128
France 38, 77

G
German Democratic Republic 67
Germany 66
Great Britain 29

H
Hawaii 62
Holland 38
Hong Kong 58, 64

I
Italy 99, 122
Ivrea 89

J
Japan 58, 59, 62, 110, 135

L
Linz 104
London XII, 5, 6, 14, 106, 107, 122,
    123, 128, 139
    Kensington High Street 5
    King's Road 1, 15, 106, 107
    Piccadilly Circus 107
    Savile Row 135
    Tailors' street 135
    markets 107
    tailors' street 135
Los Angeles 9, 48, 123
Lyon 47, 128

M
Milan 26, 89, 99, 122, 128, 139
    Via Montenapoleone 139
Minneapolis 83

N
Netherlands 46, 53, 142, 143, 146
New York 9, 12, 26, 52, 58, 64, 83,
    88, 112, 114, 116, 117, 121, 139
    Chelsea district 106, 114, 119
    Fifth Avenue 83, 91
    Manhattan Soho 114, 117
    Wooster street 121
    boutique 9

P
Pacific 58
Paris 12, 18, 26, 39, 48, 52, 55, 58,
    73, 77, 116, 117, 120, 121, 123,
    128
    16th arrondissement 79

R
Reykjavik 114
Rotterdam 146

S
San Francisco 9
Scheveningen 146
Seattle 82
Seoul 63
Sidney 48
Singapore 114
South Africa 58

T
The Hague 146
Tokyo 58, 64, 110, 112, 116, 117,
    120, 121
    Omotesando Avenue 63, 117
    Shibuya 112

U
United Kingdom 106
United States of America 2, 3, 8, 24,
    42, 82, 83, 88, 89, 114, 135

V
Vienna 18, 71, 94
    Graben Boulevard 71, 73
    Kohlmarkt 96

W
Warsaw 114

10 Corso Como 26, 122, 123, 124, 126
10 Corso Como store 123
2012 Architecten 146
6a Architects 134, XII

A
Aboriginal theme 143
agnès b. 12
American Institute of Architects 96
AMO 9
Aoki, Jun 9, 57, 60, 63
Aoyama shop 117
Apple 4
Architectural Forum 83
Arco 99
Art Club 106
Art Nouveau 89
Ashley, Laura 6
Australian 143, 144, 145
Australian Homemade 142, 143
Australian's urban archetype 143
Austrian-Hungarian court 73

B
Bakker, Gijs 129
Bally 77, 81
Bally shoe shop 28, 77
Bally shop 77
Banana Republic 8
Banfi, Gian Luigi 88
Banham, Reyner 91
Barillet, Louis 77
BBPR 91, 93
Beatles 4
Belgiojoso, Lodovico B. 88, 89
Benetton 6, 8
Benjamin, Walter 2
Bergdorf Goodman department store 112
Berlin shop 119
Best, George 4
Biba 5
Bon Marché 18, 28
Boy, Teddy 107

C
Camper 26, 30, 138, 139
Camper commercial spaces 139
Camper history 139
Camper philosophy 139
Camper stores 139
Camper's shops 139
Carlson, Eric X, 55
Casabella 89
Castiglioni, Achille 99, 100, 104
Castiglioni, Pier Giacomo 99, 100, 104

CEO 62
CFO 62
Chanel, Coco 4, 5, 15
Chelsea drugstore 106
Chelsea Football Club 107
Chloé 117
Clark, Ossie 106
Cock, Jan de 117
Colette 26, 27, 123
Comme des Garçon's products 117, 121
Comme des Garçons 15, 30, 114, 117
Comme des Garçons SHIRT 114, 117, 121
Comme des Garçons shop 119
Concrete Architectural Associates 142, 143
Connor, David 106
Conrad shop 122
Conrad, Terence 122

D
Das Andere 1903 71
Dayton's Southdale Mall 83
Dean, James 107
Dior 60
Dover Street Market 117, 123
Dresdner Molkerei Gebrüder Pfund 66
Droog Design 129
Duchi 27
Duchi shoe shop 146
Duck, Mandarina 128, 130

E
Eiffel, Gustave 18
Ellington, Duke 112

F
Ferrari, Paolo 99
Flos 42, 99, 104
Flos boutique 23
Flos showroom 99
Ford, Tom 9
Formica 98
Forum Design 104
French Revolution 39
Frisbi 99
Future Systems 114, 115, 121

G
Galerie de Bois 39
German mannerist Renaissance 69
Gesamtkunstwerk 98
Grayson 24, 32, 42, 82, 83, 86
Gruen 83, 86
Gruen, Victor 82, 83
G-Star 46, 47, 48, 53

G-Star concept 48
G-Star environment 53
G-Star Raw 48
G-Star Raw Store 47
G-Star Store 48, 53
Gucci 9
Guerrilla shop 119, 121
Guerrilla store 15, 30, 114, 119
Guixé, Marti 139

H
Helleu, Jacques 9
Henry, Hélène 77
Hermès 60
Herzog and de Meuron 9, 60
Higo & Associates 58
History of Building Types 38
Hoffmann 98
Hollein, Hans 94, 96, 98
How High the Moon 112
Hulanicki, Barbara (Biba) 4, 5

I
Ikea 23
Industrial Revolution 41

K
Kawakubo, Rei 15, 114, 115, 117,
    119, 121
Kawakubo's boutiques 117
Kawasaki, Takao 114, 115, 121
Kelly, Ben 106
Kensington Market 117
Klein, Calvin 117
Kni_e 18, 20, 23, 71
Kni_e clientele 74
Kni_e Company 73
Kni_e shop 73
Kondo, Yasuo 114
Koolhaas, Rem 9
Krummeck, Elsie 82, 83, 86
Kuma 60
Kuramata, Shiro 110, 112

L
Lang, Helmut 10
Let It Rock 106, 107
Look Back in Anger 106
Loos, Adolf 71, 73, 74
Louis Vuitton damier pattern 63
Lupi, Italo 99
LV 56, 60, 62
LV Architecture 63
LV Architecture Department 55, 56
LV brand strategy 60
LV monogram 62
LV offices 58
LV products 63

LVMH (Louis Vuitton Moët
    Hennessy) 8, 12, 55
Lydon, John 107

M
MacLaren, Malcolm 15, 106, 107
Macy's 10
Mallet-Stevens, Robert 77, 79, 80
Mandarina 129
Mandarina concept 129
Mango 117
McDonald's 56
McNulty, David 55, 56
Milliron 83
Miyake boutique 112
Miyake, Issey 110, 112
Miyake's fashion 112
Mori, Toshiko 114
Moss 12, 14
MTV 10

N
Nagoya project 57, 63
net-à-porter (.com) 14
New York Prada store 10
Nivola, Costantino 93
NL architects 128

O
Oki-ni consumer 134
Oki-ni shop 134
Oki-ni XII, 14, 26, 134, 135
Olivetti showroom 91
Olivetti, Camillo 88, 89, 91, 93
OMA 9, 60
Omotesando store 64
Ornament and Crime 1908 71
Osaka project 57

P
Palais-Royal 39
Paradise Garage 107
Parentesi 99
Paris for Perfumes 120
Parisian 'embassy' 129
Paul Gustav Leander Pfund
    (1849–1923) 66
Paxton's Crystal Palace 39
Peressutti, Enrico 88, 89
Pevsner, Nicolaus 38
Pfund dairy shop 43
Pfund, Paul 66, 67, 69
Pfunds Molkerei 66
Piano, Renzo 60
Porta Garibaldi railway station 123
Prada 9, 10, 12, 26, 60, 64, 117
Prada building 64
Prada, Miuccia 12

Prada's boutique 31
Prada's New York boutique 10

Q
Quant, Mary 4, 5, 106

R
R.S. Reynolds Memorial Award 96
Ramakers, Renny 129
Rap 11
recyclicity.net 146
Retti 28, 98
Retti candle shop 94
Retti, Marius 96
Rhode, Zandra 4
Roberts, Tommy (Mister Freedom) 4
Rogers, Ernesto N. 88, 89
Rolling Stones 106
Roodnat, Stijn 130
Roppongi shop 60
Rotten, Johnny 107
Ruhs, Kris 122

S
Salomon, André 77
Schilling, Oep X, 46
Seditionaries 106, 107, 108
Segal, Fred 123
Seibu department store 110, 112
Sejima, Kazuyo 9, 60
SEX 4, 15, 106, 107, 108
Sex Pistols 107
Smith, Paul 4

Sozzani, Carla 122, 124
Sozzani, Franca 124
Studio BBPR 88, 89
Studio KRD 117
Studio X Design Group 129

T
The Gap 8, 117
The Rocky Horror Show 106
Tiffany 10
Too Fast to Live Too Young to Die
106, 107

V
Valerie Solana's S.C.U.M. Manifesto
107
Velasca tower 89
Venini 93
Villeroy & Boch 66, 69, 70
Vinci, Leonardo da 93
Vogue Italia 124
Vuitton, Louis 9, 12, 55, 62

W
Westwood, Vivienne 4, 15, 106, 107
Wolff, Fritz 73
World's End 15, 106, 107, 108

Y
Yoox 14

Z
Zara 117

A

aboriginal patterns 145
accessibility 43
acrylic 110
act of payment 24
advertisement 9, 98
advertising 4, 9, 11, 16, 44
aggressive 9
and promotion 6
   traditional 119
aficionado 12
aisles 24
American
   consumer society XII
   society: car shoppers 86
amphitheatre 86
annual sales 62
arcade 1, 2, 3, 38, 39, 41
Arcades Project 2
architect 10, 18, 44, 58, 59, 62, 63,
      64, 71, 79, 89, 96, 99, 114, 128,
      129, 147
   external 59
architectural
arrangements 18
   continuity 63
   decisions 64
   design 48, 52
   device 117
   factors 56
   issues 56
   statements 96
   trick 76
architecturally sophisticated 62
architecture from waste 146
areas
   non-commercial 119
   non-retail 64
   focus 129
armaments 3
Art Deco motifs 5
art
   exhibition 117
   gallery 121, 134
   in retail 117
Art Nouveau motifs 5
atmosphere 104, 108
attentive service 42
Audi 100 windscreens 149
authenticity 42, 145
avant-garde 91
architecture 31
   outlook 115

B

back offices 20
bar 123
baroque architecture 96

Best-Seller Shops 139
bike straps 130
black MDF 52
bookshop 121, 126
botiga 35
boutique 1, 2, 3, 4, 5, 6, 7, 9, 10, 11,
      12, 14, 15, 17, 19, 24, 26, 27, 35,
      38, 42, 43, 55, 80, 112, 124, 134
   classic street-front 112
   concept 4
   high street 6
   idea 12
   luxury 18
   multi-brand 129
   Quant 5
   record 26
   space 81
   tailor-making 135
   super 9
brand 8, 9, 16, 24, 32, 56, 99, 116,
      119, 129
boutique 8
   identity 9, 53, 58
   image 48, 53
   image of nature 139
   luxury 8, 9, 10, 11
   merchandising 116
brushed steel 121
building
   constraints 57
   envelope 135
   process 147
   regulations 63
built-in
   cupboards 76
   displays 67
   furniture system 74
   lighting 81
buy online 134

C

café 17, 41, 66, 70, 126
candelabra-like columns 69
car shoppers 86
carpeted floors 81
cash
   area 134
counter 80
   desk 39, 52, 62, 67, 133, 149
   register 24, 121
cast iron structures 39
ceiling 73
   fittings 100
   panelled 69
   patterns 76
   sculptural 121
central courtyard 126
ceramic tiles 69

chain store model 42
chandeliers 69
changing rooms 112, 135
chrome-plated
columns 112
   steel 98
   flawless finishing 112
city patterns 38
client 42, 44, 59, 64, 74
   recruitment 26
commensurability 17
commerce 35
commercial
   demands 60
   empire 66
   environment 55
   exchange 16, 17
   interiors 77
   mall 41
   relationship 24
   retail architecture 64
   space 16
   strategy 31, 43
communication 38, 42, 44 139
concept
   shop 122
   stores 117
conceptual
   art 31
   factors 62
concrete 52, 63
   box 114
construction 58
   materials 38
   management teams 58
Consulates 128
consumer 4, 8, 30
   behaviour 16
   future 30
   group 8
   new 86
consumerism 5
consumption patterns 16
contemporary
Camper shops 139
   media 126
   retail environments 35
Corners 129
corporate identity 143
corridor 112
cosmopolitan shoppers 123
counter 20, 39, 67
craftsmanship 93, 98, 144
craftsmen 77
credit card 31, 62
cultural
   artefact 117
changes 43

connotations 108
constraints 57
   field 117
   references 126
culture 124
   approach 62
cupboard 76
   walls 87
curtain 20, 133
customer 10, 20, 31, 48, 53, 137, 149
curiosity 119
   feedback 26
   fidelity strategy 28
   high-income 135
   loyalty 28
   price-conscious 22
   recruitment 27, 28
   would-be 30
customization 10

D
dairy
   firm 66
   products 67, 69
   shop 66
damier
   motif 63
   pattern 63
décor 11
decorative
   arts 77
   arts rules 81
   elements 96
   interior 81
   qualities 69
demonstration tables 93
denim wall 52, 53
department store 3, 5, 6, 18, 23, 24,
   38, 41, 74, 112, 113, 129, 135
design 52, 64, 89
   gallery 123
   store 12, 126
designer 42, 44, 73, 99
desk 87
   cash 39, 52, 62, 67, 133, 149
   information 104
   office 104
   pay 140, 112
   reception 91
display 9, 38, 42, 43, 44, 52, 53, 74,
   76, 81, 87, 99, 104, 105, 112,
   120, 127, 133, 135, 139
   area 135
   built-in 67
   cages 9
   counter 145
   elements 69, 87, 93, 98, 105, 121,
   137, 140, 145

incubator 133
  shelves 81
  space 100
  surface 86
  tables 87
  technique 43, 44, 104
  window 53
distribution 41
division of space 115
domestic character 76
door 20
  frame 79
doorway 96
dressing rooms 74
dummy stone walls 104
dust-proof fabric 104
Dutch
  collective 129
  ground-level architecture 144
  landscapes 69
  shop 143

E
early Minimalism 117
ecological
  brand image 139
  statement 146
economic
  changes 43
  intermediation 22
  intermediation functions 24
  performance 33
economical tool 140
electronic tracking 26
electronically identifying 26
Embassies 128
entrance 63, 74, 80, 93, 108, 117,
    131, 137
  corridor 80
  door 79, 108
  to the store 44
  tunnel 115
entryway 17, 28
environments without scale 121
ephemeral
  area 30
  installation 134
Epicenters 9
ergonomics 93
e-shop 44, 134
evolution of consumer culture 4
experience
  halls 115
  shopping 18
eye level 80

F
façade 44, 53, 56, 57, 59, 60, 63, 64,
    74, 76, 79, 80, 81, 86, 107, 108,
    109, 117, 119, 139, 140
  aluminium-plated 96
  closed 120
  concealed 120
  double 63
  functions 98
  glass 63
  layered 63
  liquid 63
  moiré glass 63
  mosaic-tile 63
  polished-metal 63
  stone 63
  woven-metal 63
face-to-face contact 25
fairs 53
fashion 60, 117, 124
  magazine 14
  outlet 3
  shop 12
  techniques 112
felt sheets 137
fibreglass rods 130, 133
fitting
  elements 76
  rooms 52
fittings 89, 100, 104, 128, 145
  ceiling 100
  lighting 99, 100, 104, 139
  wall 100
flexible 60
  environment 99
floor 73
  layout 43
  tiles 67
fluo-cupboards 133
franchise 42, 32
  outlets 42
  stores 42
freedom to choose 5
front
  door 74
  offices 20
furniture 53, 60, 124, 130
  domestic 127
  island-like 121
  office 89
  steel 114

G
gallery 117, 126
  design 123
gelateria 144, 145

generic
    retail space 35
    shop 35
glass 18, 38, 79, 110
    crown 38
    double layer of printed 63
    façade 63
    leaded 38
    plate 38
    screens 67
    walls 9
    white flashed opal 108
    window 81
glazed
    shop fronts 38
    showcases 74
glossy
    magazine 14
    publications 124
graffiti 10
grainy tan-coloured quartz ceramic
    104
grand salon 80, 81
granite 67
    pillars 74
Great War (1914–18) 1
guidelines 31
guild system 39

H
hand-painted tiles 69
hanging lamps 93
High Street 106
honeycomb panels 105

I
identity 53, 56, 99
image 53, 56, 64
imitates silver 79
impulsive shopping 98
industrial
    designers 44, 77
    materials 110
industrialization 18
in-store devices 22, 24
instruction cards 139, 140
insulation chamber 100
interiorization 98
Internet 14, 15, 44
    site 14
inverse clothes rack 133
Italian design 89

L
laboratories 53
labyrinth-like space 104

laminate shelves 104
leather armchairs 76
leftover spaces 64, 135
leisure activity 32
liberation of shopkeepers 39
lifestyle 3, 122, 124
light 53, 112
    diffusion 105
    effects 104
    incandescent 86
    natural 100, 127
    neon 108
    source 100
lighting 18, 31, 53, 44, 86, 139, 145
    artificial 100
    basic 86, 87
    built-in 81
    cold 145
    cold and harsh 17
    concealed 93
    device 79
    electric 38
    fittings 99, 100, 104, 139
    fluorescent 86
    fluorescent neon 137
    general 137
    reflector for 81
    self-supporting system 133
    soft 137
    techniques 87
    traditional (incandescent) 86
    warm 145
limited edition 27
listening areas 26
location 6, 31, 41, 42, 43, 52, 53, 62,
    119, 134, 135
    choice of 117
    prime 117
    specific 120, 143
logo 32
low culture 11
luxury 18, 115, 121
    bazaar 117
    boutiques 18
    brands 8, 9, 10, 11
    goods 3, 55
    retail 60, 62, 64
    retail sector 60
    retail neighbourhoods 59
    retailer 12, 64

M
magasin 35
magazines 6, 56, 130, 137
    fashion 14
    glossy 14

mail-order service 6
mainstream
  companies 117
market 48
Mandarina concept 129
market 16, 25, 31, 53, 135
  function 31
  identity 26
  intermediation 16, 17
  intermediation forces 17
  leader 91
mechanism 25
mediation 20, 25, 32
medium 32
  placement strategies 6
  relationship 17, 18, 19, 24, 28, 31,
    32
  space 16, 17, 31
  stall 38
  strategy 8
  techniques 25
marketing
  instrument 24
  strategy 25, 27
  tool 39, 130, 140
marketplace 6, 8
Marshall Plan 3
mass
  culture 86
market 2, 5, 6, 8, 9, 11, 12, 15, 86
market merchandisers 9
marketplace 6
media outlets 6
  produced artefact 9
  production 18, 145
  public 9
  publicity 9
  tourism 70
materials 42, 44, 60, 62, 91, 115
  cheap 108
  construction 58
  discarded 147
  industrial 110
mix of 63
  second-hand 109
  recyclable 14, 56, 139, 147
  traditional 73
MDF 140
media 117
  exposure 115
merchandising 16, 52, 53, 60, 63, 145
  brand 116
  visual 52
merchant identity 32
metal 112
  boxes 137
  openwork 112

metallic
  arches 112
  exterior 81
  paintwork 105
  structures 18
minimalism 121
mirror 73, 76, 81, 98, 121
  gilded 69
  industry 38
mixed gravel tiles 112
modernism 91
moiré effect 63, 112
monolithic marble blocks 93
movable cases 100
multi-brand
  boutiques 129
  environments 47
  outlets 47
  retail points 47
museum-like setting 27

N
neglected areas 119
neo-classical architecture 96
Neoliberty 89, 93
neutral background 73
niches 87, 121
nickel-silver plates 80

O
oak floor 135
office
  desk 104
  environment 93
  furniture 89
  space 91
off-the-shelf shop-fitting equipment
  8
online
  retailer 26
order 137
orange shantung 98
ornament 71
ornamentation 73, 91
orthodox rationalism 91
outlet 4, 5, 6, 9, 10, 35, 48, 115
  fashion 3
  franchise 42
  mass media 6
  multi-brand 47
  retail 2, 9, 12, 26, 53
  temporary 119

P
packaging 16, 145
painting on white-plastered walls 81
pallet tunnel 133

partitions 20
passages 143
passer-by 28, 98
pay
    area 74, 76
    cash 25
    desk 140, 112
paying zone 98
payment 25
    operations 24, 25
procedures 26
pedestals 93
pedestrian
    areas 143
    lanes 39
pin wall 133
pink
    Candoglia marble 93
padded plastic 108
plastered walls 121
plastic laminate 104, 105
plates of chromed nickel-silver 79
plywood construction 149
polished aluminium 98
post-war period 91
prêt-à-porter 14
price tag 28
private spheres 43
product 31, 32, 53, 64, 98, 116, 130
    atmosphere 122
    based innovations 39
    design 16
    information 22
    line 56
positioning 25
public
    area 41, 62
    domain 38, 117
    retail space 17
    space 31, 32, 39, 86, 93
    sphere 43, 86
publicity 9, 11, 107
pyramidal target audience 8

R
radio frequency identification (RFI)
    54
railway system 41
raw oak 52
real estate strategy 130
re-branding 42
reception
    area 39
    desk 91
recyclable 146
    materials 14, 56, 139, 147
    wood 149

representation of the market 26
restaurant 17, 123, 126
retail
    architecture 16, 17, 20, 24, 25, 26,
        30, 31, 32, 71
    architecture's efficiency 33
    chains 8
    element 73
    environments 8
    formula 122
    groups 8
    luxury 60, 62, 64
    outlet 2, 9, 12, 26, 53
    points 129
relationship 19
    space 17, 25, 30, 62
    specialist 86
    strategy 10
    techniques 86
rib mesh 112
routing 24

S
sale surface 39
sales 42, 43
    department 52
    interaction 26
    per square metre 52
    person 22
    psychology reasons 96
    techniques 43
scene 29, 30
Second Word War (1939–45) 2, 22,
    86
security fences 117
self-service 22, 24, 25, 44
selling
    area 41, 98
    point 9, 107, 115
space 35, 80
service 18, 35, 124
    access 63
    window 20, 28
shadow effects 105
shelves 24, 112, 121, 133
    mobile 67
shoeboxes 139, 140
shoemaker 139
shop 1, 2, 3, 4, 6, 9, 10, 12, 17, 22,
    25, 26, 27, 28, 31, 35, 38, 41, 42,
    53, 55, 64, 116, 134
    anti 115
    area 32
    assistant 24
    butcher 25
    closed 18
    concept 122, 133

dairy 66
designers 44
fashion 12
front 8, 39, 147
generic 35
interactive 139
interior 54, 67
mono-brand 47
off-centre 119
owner 25
permanent 139
sign 27, 39, 79
signage 8
small-scale 38, 42
specialist 2
speciality 35, 41, 43
staff 20
temporary 139
traditional 24
window 32, 38, 44, 67, 69, 74, 76,
79, 80, 86, 98, 108, 133, 135,
139, 149
window closed 98
shop's
architect 25
salons 23
shop-in-shop 43, 112
shopkeeper 139, 140
shopkeeper's household 41
shopping
action 139
experience 10, 63
mall 2, 6, 24, 83, 143
mall environment 112
mall regional 6
street 143
showcase 76, 80, 135
showroom 28, 53, 91, 100, 112
silent salesmen 39
site-specific approach 62
skin 63
small profit and quick return 28
smooth tiled surface 69
sneak preview 30
social
activity 86
changes 107
class 20
codes 19
distinctions 19
interactions 26, 35
issues 42, 43
movements 44
programmes 66
role 107
status 32
Space Age 5

space
divider 133
semi-public 32
spatial 56
boundaries 20
concept 52
conditions 59
distinction 52
division 149
experience 62
square 38, 143
S-shaped stands 104
stage 25, 29, 48
design 135
stainless steel 145
structure 149
staircase 131
stairs 57
stands 53
steel
black 52
furniture 114
mesh 110
untreated 52
stock 62
management 54
room 149
stone tiles 113
storage 42, 74, 81, 134, 140
shelf 147, 149
area 98, 112, 135
containers 98
place 35
store 41, 64
chain 25, 32, 35, 42, 43, 86
Committee 62
concept 117
design 12, 126
flagship 55, 64, 127, 128
franchise 42
front 28, 32
grocery 22, 29
interiors 57
pre-fabricated 30
sizes 56
street culture 10
subdivision of space 98
suburban
arcades 41
strip/scale area 86
supermarket 17, 22, 24

T
table lamps 100
target
audience 8
group 43, 139

theatrical interiors 24
three-dimensional
  catalogues 23
  fashion magazine 124
thresholds 98
tiles 70
trade fairs 53
  33rd Milan 104
traditional
  advertising 119
  atmosphere 119
  characteristics 42
  commerce 28
  division 81
  materials 73
shop 24
shopping areas 124
  trajectories 31
  transactions 24
  transgressive spaces 20
  translucent polycarbonate pallets
    133
  travertine-clad walls 86
  tribal identification 10
  trihedrons 104
  trying-out element 147
  typology 38, 64

U
urban
archetype 143
footprint 38
landscape 106

V
vertical market groupings 8
vintage elements 108
VIP room 62
visual
  distortion 63
  merchandising 52

W
Walk in Progress 139
  shop 139
  store138
wall 73, 139
  fittings 100
  tiles 67
  paper 9
warehouse 12
webpages 14
website 12, 14, 26
white
  cube 10
  plastic laminate 100
window 18, 27, 38
  displays 63
  glass 81
  service 20, 28
  side 112
wooden
  built-in cupboards 73
  door 93
  panelling 81
  partition 62
wrapping zone 98
Wunderkammer 12

Printed in Great Britain
by Amazon